Praise for
WOWABILITY—How to Achieve It & Why It Matters

A must read for entrepreneurs and anyone managing established brands as *Wowability* allows you to stay at the top and build a legacy.

M.A. Venkataramanan, Ph.D.
Chairperson, Undergraduate Programs
Kelley School of Business
Indiana University

Wowability is a refreshing newcomer to an otherwise tired bookshelf. Drawing on Imran Syed's excellent insights and various relevant case studies, *Wowability* is a fun blueprint for brands that want to stand out from the crowd. Grab it, and prepare to say, "Wow!"

Ian Stewart
Senior Vice President
MTV Networks International

Wowability provides a fresh perspective on how to build powerful brands. It is a must read for marketing professionals who want to build the top brand in their space!

Dr. Jochen Wirtz
Associate Professor of Marketing
Co-Director of the UCLA-NUS Executive MBA
National University of Singapore

In his book, Imran Syed has captured the essence of branding— Wowability. In addition to introducing this revolutionary approach to branding, Syed also elaborates further on how to achieve and sustain preferred status among clients. Wow! I would definitely recommend this book to all our students.

Petra Turkama
Director, Executive Education
Helsinki School of Economics

Not all brands have the wherewithal or the know-how to become "Wowable." The first, essential step is for brand owners to be proactive in creating Wowability. Imran Syed challenges us all to exceed expectations, and gives a practical and digestible way for brand owners to know "How to Wow."

Craig Briggs
Managing Director, Asia
Desgrippes Gobe Group

In our current dynamic world, where competition knows no boundaries, Wowability is everything! Imran Syed's thought leadership on this subject is amazing. Don't miss this future classic.

Ven Raman
Managing Director, India and South East Asia
Carl Zeiss

Wowability is an amazing and powerful concept—underpinned by logic, proof points, principles, and insights—making this a must-read for all stakeholders of a brand

Deepika Nikhilender
Regional Managing Partner
MindShare Asia Pacific

The powerful concept of Wowability, along with a set of coherent framework and tools, make this book a must-read for anyone interested in creating and sustaining successful brands. The author draws from his rich experience and enlightening research to make a complex subject easy to understand and highly actionable. I highly recommend this book!

Tan Kim Leng
Managing Director, KDi Asia Pte Ltd
President, Nanyang MBA Alumni Association (2005 – 2007)

!
WOW

WOWABILITY
wowowowowowowowowowowowowowowowowowowowowowowowowowowowowowowowowowow
How To Achieve It & Why It Matters

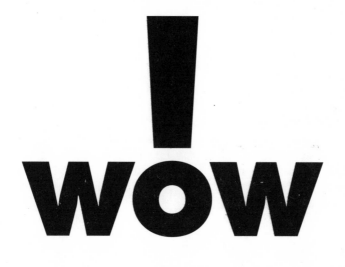

WOWABILITY

How To Achieve It & Why It Matters

Imran Syed

WILEY

John Wiley & Sons (Asia) Pte. Ltd.

Copyright © 2008 by Imran Syed
Published in 2008 by John Wiley & Sons (Asia) Pte. Ltd.
2 Clementi Loop, #02-01, Singapore 129809

This publication is designed to provide accurate and authoritative
information in regard to the subject matter covered. It is sold with the
understanding that the publisher or the author is not engaged in rendering
professional services. If professional advice or other expert assistance is
required, the services of a professional should be sought.

Other Wiley Editorial Offices

John Wiley & Sons, 111 River Street, Hoboken, NJ 07030, USA
John Wiley & Sons, The Atrium Southern Gate, Chichester P019 8SQ,
    England
John Wiley & Sons (Canada) Ltd., 5353 Dundas Street West, Suite 400,
    Toronto Ontario M9B 6HB. Canada
John Wiley & Sons Australia Ltd. 42 McDougall Street, Milton,
    Queensland 4064, Australia
Wiley-VCH, Bosch Strasse 12, D-69469 Weinheim, Germany

Library of Congress Cataloging-in-Publication Data

ISBN 978-0-470-82289-0

Typeset in 11/15 Points ITC Novarese by JC Ruxpin Pte. Ltd.
Printed in Singapore by Saik Wah Press Ltd.
10 9 8 7 6 5 4 3 2 1

DEDICATION

Dedicated to my family

AUTHOR'S PLEDGE

The author has pledged to donate part of the proceeds from this book to The Grameen Foundation, a nonprofit organization that aims to alleviate global poverty by giving microloans for entrepreneurship to some of the world's poorest families. This is based on the microfinance strategy initiated by 2006 Nobel Peace Prize Laureate Professor Muhammad Yunus. The author believes this to be the best way to end global poverty. Give a family a fish and you feed them for a day, give them the resources to fish and you feed them for life.

TABLE OF CONTENTS

ACKNOWLEDGMENTS   ix

FOREWORD   xi

PREFACE   xiii

CHAPTER 1   5
Introduction to Wowability

CHAPTER 2   15
Brand Banking

CHAPTER 3   31
The Economics of Wowability

CHAPTER 4   47
Contact Points

CHAPTER 5   63
Functional Contact Points

CHAPTER 6   85
Emotional Contact Points

CHAPTER 7   111
Communicational Contact Points

CHAPTER 8   137
Quantitative Tools

CHAPTER 9   165
Qualitative Tools

CHAPTER 10   179
Sustaining Wowability

CHAPTER 11   197
    Principles of Wowability and the Way Ahead

APPENDIX I   207
    Wowability Surveys

APPENDIX II   211
    The Wowability Framework

ENDNOTES   219

INDEX   235

ACKNOWLEDGMENTS

I am truly grateful to the entire Asatsu-DK (ADK) organization, particularly Masao Inagaki and Koichiro Naganuma, for supporting me and this book. I would also like to thank Osamu Ishikawa and Masato Hori for their endless encouragement, and Kazuki Shiobara, Charlie Gan, and Fang-Teo Hup Choo for their guidance and suggestions.

My thanks also go to my staff and assistants: Alex Tan, Jannell Lee, Jing Ting Ng, Norisha Ridzwan, Visayon Viravong, and Wan Lin Chew. Furthermore, I would like to express my gratitude to the MBA students of the SPJ Center of Management, Singapore: Aditya Bansal, Akshat Dimri, Amit Mehta, Indranil Puzari, Jaydeep Hingne, Joydeb Mukherjee, Nisha Koshy, Saipriya Rajagopalan, Shahid Mohamed, and Tushar Ranjan, for their contribution to the Wowability framework and its successful implementation through the "Wowability Consulting Group."

I would like to take this opportunity to thank C.J. Hwu, Janis Soo, Joel Balbin, Nick Wallwork, Mark Allin, and the other members of the John Wiley Asia team for their faith in me. I appreciate your patience and guidance, without which this book would have forever remained a jumble of bits and bytes inside my notebook.

I would like to thank my family: Although spread across multiple countries, you remain very close to my heart. I would like to thank you, Mom, for raising me the best way a mother can, and thank you, Dad, for instilling in me your creativity. I would also like to thank my wife, Feng-Miao, who lovingly bears with all my whims. I would like to thank my sisters, Ambereen and Meenaz, for their loving support. I would like to wish eternal happiness and success to my son, Brandon, who has changed my life for the better. I am also grateful for the love I've received from my family in-law: Dad, Hsin Chu, Hsin Er, Wei Kai, and Shao Wen.

I would also like to thank my well-wishers: my friends, colleagues, professors and teachers, especially Agnello Sir and B.P. Singh.

Last but not least, I would like to thank the Almighty for giving us this wonderful life, and without whom none of this would matter.

FOREW**O**RD

For quite some time now practitioners and academics alike have tried to come up with a strategic paradigm that would allow companies to compete in today's hyper-competitive, cluttered and globalized world. Wowability is such a strategy that can help brands to become leaders today. Imran Syed has successfully created a strategic framework that can help a brand achieve the highest level of leadership possible.

I have known and interacted with Imran Syed for several years. He has a talent for creating innovative ideas that derive from his passionate desire to help his clients reach the next level. Examples of this creativity are the multiple *Meter tools* and *Worksheets* as well as the multiple paradigms and methodologies such as FAR *paradigm*, *Brand Banking* and *Wowability* that he has created. I am delighted to see that he has decided to put his thoughts and ideas into writing. His thought-leadership and clear presentation of complicated paradigms in this book are exemplary. In fact, *Wowability* rewrites the existing rules of the game.

Wowability is the type of "Big Think Strategy" that I have written about in my own recent book. For too long now companies have been focused on the short term and on mere survival. And unfortunately the vast majority of companies have no intention of wowing their consumers.

To be a leader in an industry requires being the customer's first choice. This requires that the company exceeds customers' expectations—that is, wow them. This insight into human psychology, along with the Wowability strategy that Imran provides, changes everything. In the future, companies may well be classified as those with—and those without—*Wowability*.

I hope in your own business you travel with the roadmap of Wowability.

Bernd Schmitt, PhD
Executive Director, Center on Global Brand Leadership
Professor, Columbia Business School

PREFACE

Why do people prefer some things over others? Is there a commonality among human choices? Can we pinpoint the basic reasons behind this? Can we alter the choices that people make? These questions have bothered me for a long time. My motive for seeking answers was not only to help brands sell more and become market leaders, but also to help people make better choices and reach practical solutions. This book is about what I have learned from this quest. It is about what I call *"Wowability."*

Wowability is the ability to consistently delight by exceeding expectations. This is what makes people choose some things over others. If you or your brand can consistently delight your target audience by exceeding its expectations, you will be on your way to becoming a market leader.

The way this book is structured

The book starts out with a definition of Wowability and explains why it is needed. It then breaks down branding, using the brand bank concept, and moves on to show how Wowability works, its economics, its various constituents, plus the tools and processes needed to achieve it. Besides stories on brands and companies, we will also look at ways of carrying out and sustaining Wowability. We conclude with some overall principles, a general framework, and the way ahead.

Have fun reading and email me at wowability@gmail.com with any comments or suggestions.

Imran Syed
Singapore,
April 2008

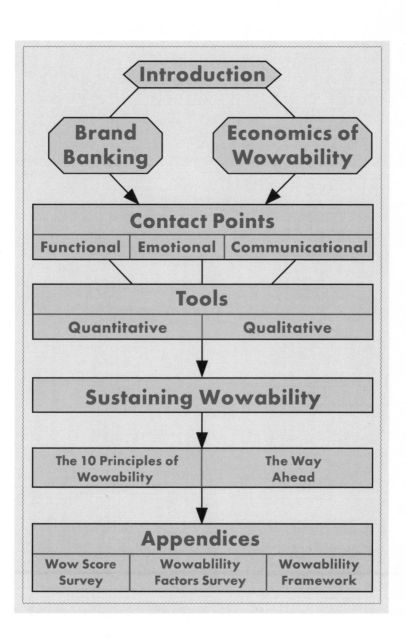

Introduction

Brand Banking

Economics of Wowability

Contact Points

| Functional | Emotional | Communicational |

Tools

| Quantitative | Qualitative |

Sustaining Wowability

| The 10 Principles of Wowability | The Way Ahead |

Appendices

| Wow Score Survey | Wowablility Factors Survey | Wowablility Framework |

!

**"So inscrutable is
the arrangement of causes
and consequences in this
world that a two-penny
duty on tea, unjustly
imposed in a sequestered
part of it, changes the
condition of all its
inhabitants."** [1]

– Thomas Jefferson, (*referring to Boston Tea party*)

chapter 1

What is Wowability?

People prefer certain brands over others. In fact some brands receive first preference from many people. This is due to Wowability. Successful brands like Samsung, Apple, Starbucks, Toyota, Nokia, and Coca-Cola all have Wowability, and so they lead their fields in market share while earning extraordinary profits.

One opinion is that it takes exceptional talent or charisma, like that of Steve Jobs, Bill Gates, or Richard Branson, to create brands like Apple, Microsoft, and Virgin. But these brands did not become great simply by having celebrity CEOs. They became great because they had Wowability. So what exactly is Wowability?

Wowability is the ability to consistently delight by exceeding expectations.

The key points are to consistently delight and to exceed expectations. It is easy to understand either concept individually, but to maintain focus on and implement both ideas is not just a matter of understanding them in theory. To achieve Wowability, a brand has to deliver more than what its consumers expect. And the extra effort of going beyond consumer expectations must ultimately delight the consumer. Consumers must also be consistently delighted if the brand is going to retain its customer base.

This book strives to explain and illustrate how companies can achieve Wowability. But first let us elaborate on why achieving Wowability is important.

Merely satisfying customer needs is no longer enough, especially as globalization and technological advances have increased competition in many markets. A student can now buy books over the internet if prices there are cheaper than those at his local bookstore. A car dealer, meanwhile, can check the prices of cars on his competitor's website and then base his own prices on what he learns. The internet has made product information more accessible to the public, and comparisons are easily made with a few clicks of the mouse. All this has resulted in lower profit margins and ugly price wars across industries.

If a brand wants to appeal to the broader market, it needs to offer greater value for the consumer's buck. According to Bob Harris, President of the consumer relations consultancy Attrition Busters, a satisfied customer is eight times more likely to switch to a competitor than a delighted customer.[2] Merely satisfying your customer means delivering the expected value, which, over time, leads to boredom, and the customer starts looking elsewhere.

However, if a brand delivers more value than consumers expect, continually delighting them, then it may well have won itself a loyal customer.

There are simply far too many brands in the market today. By the beginning of this decade, the number of brands in

American grocery stores had tripled to 45,000[3] from a decade earlier. Brand information also proliferates outside grocery stores and the average consumer is bombarded with so much information that he has become desensitized. It is now more crucial, yet more difficult, to rise above the clutter. Having Wowability will automatically allow a brand to do this. When a brand consistently exceeds expectations, its customers become loyal consumers.

Why does exceeding expectations work?

Companies have existing philosophies on how to generate a healthy bottom line. As a result of these philosophies, catch phrases, such as "lower costs," "push sales," and others have plagued employees. However, these creeds are often reactive or limited to a specific group of people in the company. The philosophy of exceeding expectations, on the other hand, is proactive and brings together the entire group of stakeholders behind the brand and makes them think about what their consumers expect, and how to exceed those expectations.

Think of some of the most successful brands, and you will realize that all have exceeded expectations in some way or another. Starbucks, for example, has delighted us with the amount of attention paid to product quality and customer service. Others exceed expectations on different fronts: Coca-Cola with its advertising, iPod with its design and simplicity, Nokia with its design and performance, and the list goes on.

It is a fact that consumers have a set of expectations for all the products and services they use. If you do not exceed these expectations, there is no real reason for consumers to choose your brand. If your brand is neither the cheapest nor the most stylish nor the most practical or easiest to use, why should a consumer choose it over something else? Put yourself in the shoes of the consumer and be brutally honest.

There are a host of brands cluttering the market, but the vast majority of these are mediocre, and your brand can rise above them to become the top brand in its field. Whether it does, however, depends on what you do to make sure that your brand achieves Wowability. This is the only way to become a "super-brand." When your brand starts exceeding expectations, it achieves Wowability, and your brand name turns into an exceptional brand promise. In the spring of 2006, I conducted primary studies at Asatsu-DK (ADK) that found a strong statistical correlation between exceeding expectations and factors like preference and delight. Please refer to the Wowability Factors Survey in Appendix 1 for more information on the methodology and brief results of the study.

A brand promise can be achieved even without a "brand name." In the 1980s, a store by the name of Mujirushi Ryohin opened in Japan.[4] The name means "No brand, Good product." Muji's core philosophy was to create a no-brand retail space. This was a tough sell in the brand-conscious Japanese market.

Did the brand-loving Japanese consumers avoid shopping at this no-brand store? No. Curiosity pulled people into the store, and they tried its products. Consumers were "Wow-ed" by how affordable the products were without sacrificing quality. They had not expected to get such quality at the prices they were paying. Muji achieved Wowability. Over time, the store's reputation spread as shoppers recommended it to others, helping it to grow to over 300 outlets worldwide in just 20 years.[5] Muji now enjoys first preference status with many consumers. The "No brand, Good product" store has become a "good" brand in itself. Exceeding expectations definitely works for brands— even when there is no brand.

Brands have succeeded for a variety of reasons. McDonald's is successful because of its efficiency, cleanliness, ubiquitous presence, and clever marketing. Dell, on the other hand, attained success by offering quality PCs at comparatively low prices, a move made possible by its revolutionary business model. It also made PCs customizable and shortened delivery times. Each of these factors can be narrowed down to its essence, i.e., contact point. These brands have exceeded expectations in certain contact points, just like Starbucks, Coca-Cola, and other highly successful brands. **By identifying key contact points and turning them into Wow *points*, other brands can also rise above the clutter.**

The Wow Effect

In 1997, Barry Cohen, CEO of Old San Francisco, a San Antonio-based restaurant chain, spoke about using the "Wow" effect to maintain the chain's competitive edge in a cutthroat industry.[6] In this industry, 60% of new businesses fail within the first five years, and 25% don't make it past their first anniversary.[7] He referred to the "Wow" effect as what the restaurant did to create "freshness" for its customers and employees. By motivating employees, Old San Francisco's customers saw happy and passionate service personnel attending to them. This goodwill naturally spread to the customers, and happy customers in turn made it easier for the restaurant's staff to do their jobs well. Goodwill is contagious and has made Old San Francisco a wonderful place to dine, as well as to work in.

However, Cohen was aware that meeting current expectations was not enough to guarantee survival. Food quality and ambience play a major role in any restaurant's success, and Cohen paid attention to all the details, never missing an opportunity to "Wow" customers. In an industry where most fall back on tried and tested formulas, Old San Francisco has taken a different tack. Its restaurants are designed on different themes, creating a unique ambience for its customers. Patrons thus enjoy their surroundings while they enjoy their meals. Having sustained its Wowability through the 1990s even as competition intensified,[8] Old San Francisco is now positioning itself to fill many more hungry stomachs. New restaurant themes are constantly being created: Recently, a restaurant based on the 1940s opened its doors, complete with a replica of a WWII bomber. Cohen also "Wows" consumers by promoting the restaurant in different and original ways. It is not unusual for Cohen and his staff to carry trays of appetizers to random hair salons to give hairdressers and their patrons a taste of Old San Francisco.[9] He figures that hairdressers talk to about eight people per day, and this type of product placement will generate even more publicity for the chain.

Steven Spielberg's Wow Story

Wowability does not apply only to company-owned brands. As long as the entity delights and exceeds the expectations of its audience, it achieves Wowability. Steven Spielberg is a highly prolific filmmaker, having made 42 movies over a period of 46 years.[10] His movies consistently captivate audiences and win acclaim. Spielberg is an extremely discerning filmmaker. He has used some of the best technology, mostly in mechanical electronics, coupled with an astute mastery of storytelling, to add value to his movies. His movies are also often so emotionally charged that they consistently exceed the audience's expectations of a typical action or adventure film. Lesser known moviemakers have explored similar themes in the past, but it is Spielberg's movies that become classics.

E.T. is a great example. A moviegoer would naturally expect such a film to be packed with action and adventure. But after meeting these expectations, the film delighted viewers with its amazing emotional depth. Spielberg's moviemaking incorporates innovative techniques that involve the audience so much that they truly feel distressed by conflicts in the movie. In *E.T.*, Spielberg even made viewers slowly fall in love with an alien![1]

Spielberg's movies have achieved Wowability, but beyond that, Spielberg himself has Wowability. When we think we know his style and can predict what he will do next, he completely exceeds our expectations. He has made historical movies, such as *Munich* and *Schindler's List*, which are completely different from *Jaws* and *Jurassic Park*, yet they delight audiences equally. Spielberg's films are classics because they exceed our expectations of what movies should be like. Spielberg's Wowability is what sets him apart from other filmmakers.

!

"A brand for a company is like a reputation for a person. You earn reputation by trying to do hard things well."[1]

— Jeff Bezos, Founder, Amazon.com

chapter ❷

Although departments, companies, or even individuals can strive to achieve Wowability when they want to enhance their image in the eyes of their audience, it is especially valuable in the context of brands. To appreciate the value of Wowability, we must first understand how consumers perceive and understand brands. Brand banking is a simple approach that demonstrates the interplay of brands within the consumer's mind.

In general, brands play the role of identifiers and simplify the consumer's selection process. This is extremely useful today, when choices abound in almost every category. While not a bad thing, it definitely makes life complex. The key role of branding is to help us navigate this complexity.

Now let's imagine a huge consortium of banks, each with multiple accounts. Each bank represents a brand, and each account represents a specific contact point of the brand. Contact points are all experiences through which consumers directly or indirectly come in contact with, or obtain information about, the brand. They may include product quality, design, or even advertising. With this analogy in mind, let's take a look at brand banking.

The 12 Principles of Brand Banking

(1) A brand preference ladder exists in the minds of consumers for every relevant category, and brands are ranked on this ladder.

A brand preference ladder is a virtual ladder in consumers' minds that ranks brands in order of preference. When a consumer is buying a product, he mentally refers to the preference ladder for that product category, and he will usually buy the brand that is on the top rung, unless something outside his control prevents him from doing so— if that brand is out of stock, for example. As a new category becomes relevant, the consumer forms a new ladder in his mind. If a consumer wants to buy a dishwasher, for instance, he will form a ladder for this category, and will actively seek out information to rank the various dishwasher brands before making a decision. A brand enjoying first preference status will experience greater sales, higher profits, and increased consumer loyalty. This is an enviable position, and many brands strive to reach the top rung of the preference ladder.

(2) A brand bank exists in the minds of consumers for every brand they are familiar with.

As soon as consumers become familiar with a new brand, a brand bank for that brand forms in their minds. As we are continually exposed to new brands, our minds could potentially create new brand banks every day. However, brand banks are set up only for brands that we are familiar with and have information about. Brands that we are barely aware of, and those that we barely have any information about, will not have a brand bank in our minds. Hence, familiarity with a brand is important to consider when discussing the success of brands.

(3) Master brand banks exist for "mother" brands, and they affect the brand banks that fall under them through the halo effect.

Brands like Samsung, Sony, and Yamaha have a master brand bank for the main corporate brand with multiple individual brand banks under it. Take Samsung's products, for example. They are too numerous for a consumer to be familiar with them all. Consumers would typically be familiar with a few of the company's mobile phone models and perhaps one or two of its plasma television makes. So a consumer familiar with two of Samsung's mobile phone models and a particular plasma television model, but not with its other products, like its flash memory chips or computer monitors, would have just three Samsung brand banks. These three brand banks would fall under the Samsung master brand bank, which is the umbrella brand.

When Samsung advertises select mobile phone models by highlighting their unique features, such as the television output feature of the Samsung D600,[2] the brand bank accounts for these mobile phones as well as the overall master brand bank balance for Samsung are simultaneously strengthened. Due to the halo effect, a strong master brand bank would create a positive consumer perception of the other brand banks under it. Suppose a consumer is exposed to a new Samsung mobile phone model. Due to Samsung's strong master brand bank, the consumer would perceive the mobile phone favorably, even without enough information about, or experience with, that particular model.

This effectively creates a cycle: Fantastic individual brands strengthen the master brand, while new products enjoy the halo effect radiating from the master brand.

(4) A regular bank account exists for every contact point that a brand has.

Within each brand bank, there are many bank accounts representing the brand's various contact points. Coca-Cola's brand bank would have individual accounts representing contact points like taste, price, packaging, and advertising. The bank balance or the brand equity of Coca-Cola is derived from the sum of all these individual accounts.

(5) A brand's bank account can be credited or debited not only by the brand's owners but also by other brands.

Positive feelings toward a particular contact point will credit that contact point's account, while negative feelings debit the account. The overall brand bank balance ultimately depends on the balance in each individual account. In the 1990s, Nokia pushed for better design.[3] Consumers found this to be relevant and credible, thus Nokia's design contact point was credited, which boosted its overall brand bank balance. On the other hand, when the movie *Supersize Me*[4] criticized McDonald's for being the primary force behind weight gain in the U.S., consumers debited its nutritional value account, which lowered its overall brand bank balance. Competing brands can also debit each other's accounts. Because brand banks are closely connected to one another, a brand that does exceedingly well in a contact point can cause the corresponding contact point in another brand to seem worse off.

This appears clearly in comparative advertising, which highlights the superior qualities of one product over another. In fact, presidential elections in the U.S. are often better remembered for the way candidates seek to discredit one another than for the way they promote themselves. This form of advertising aims at two objectives: crediting their own brand bank accounts while simultaneously debiting competitor accounts.

With this crediting and debiting of brand bank accounts brands need to pay attention to how their actions affect their overall balances. Moreover, brands also need to understand how the actions of other brands affect them.

(6) Inactivity leads to a depreciation in the overall balance of the brand bank.

Actual banks become bankrupt when depleted of resources, but a brand bank fades from memory. Brand banks that no longer have active accounts are ultimately doomed because consumers eventually forget about the brands and the products that they have to offer.

Besides the problem of depreciation, people are also exposed to new brands everyday, and via more mediums than ever before. Billboards, store signs, internet banner advertisements, pop-up windows in cyberspace, television advertisements, and product placement all barrage consumers daily. All these communications, make matters worse for an inactive brand.

McDonald's and Coca-Cola are among the most recognizable brands globally. These brands have spent several decades and billions of dollars advertising to build brand equity. They have also constantly updated their ads to remain fresh and relevant to consumers.

But keeping brand bank accounts active does not necessarily mean constant advertising. Luxury brands like Ferrari and LVMH do not regularly advertise in the mass media since their products are often priced beyond the reach of the masses.

To prevent the brand from cooling, LVMH constantly refreshes its catalogues with new designs sporting the famous

LV initials. Louis Vuitton introduces a new collection each season, and occasionally launches super-limited edition products–like the Theda bag–to generate hype for its range of handbags. Launched in 2004, Theda bags were only available in the U.S. at the brand's Fifth Avenue store in New York. In the U.K., just 10 bags were available countrywide.[6] The company relied on Hollywood stars who carry Louis Vuitton handbags, like Angelina Jolie, to increase brand visibility.

Minimal advertising can work if key contact points are created to stimulate a desire for the company's product and are combined with less direct communications from the brand. In this case, consumers who loved the exclusivity of the Theda bag were further enticed by the lack of information available about it. This strategy requires a great deal of caution, as there is a high risk of backfiring. The key point here is that brand bank accounts need to be kept active for a brand to be healthy and growing.

(7) A brand has to continuously try to increase its bank balance.

The previous principle highlights the dangers of allowing brand bank accounts to become inactive, and leads to the seventh principle: The brand bank must continuously increase its assets by adding to its accounts. This can be done either by improving on existing contact points and crediting the corresponding brand bank account, or by adding new contact points.

To improve existing contact points, the brand can enhance design and quality as well as increase advertising. Adding new contact points may be as simple as adding a new communications medium like magazines. More complex ways to generate contact points could include promoting the Brand Leader (creating a celebrity CEO like Steve Jobs or Richard

Branson, for instance), drawing attention to an interesting history behind the brand (Disney), or provoking interest with a secret recipe (Coca-Cola).

The key to maximizing a brand's assets is to identify the contact points that are important, and to focus efforts on them. By focusing efforts on contact points that are essentially unimportant to consumers, the brand does not add significant value to its brand bank. Will a hefty investment in repackaging the product to come in different colors truly add value if the product remains essentially the same? That entirely depends on consumer perception. And so if a brand finds itself doing well in a contact point that consumers do not deem important, it should consider switching focus, or convincing consumers through marketing and communications that this contact point is important and should play a role when they are considering purchases.

One of the key contributing factors to the iPod's success was its award-winning "silhouette" advertising campaign that featured the silhouettes of people from diverse backgrounds dancing to tunes on their iPods.[7] The black silhouettes contrasted with the white iPods and the neon colors in the background for an eye-catching advertisement. Apple produced a number of versions of this ad, each featuring different characters, music, dance styles, and background colors. This increased consumer interest in the ad and held their attention longer. Furthermore, the simplicity and innovativeness of these ads complemented iPod's and Apple's images. Most advertisers focus on the "product features" brand bank account, but Apple chose to create emotional contact points like "coolness" and "freedom." It then used advertising to suggest that it was "cooler" and "freer" than its competitors. This added tremendously to the overall bank balance of the Apple and iPod brands.

(8) A higher brand bank account balance will result in a move up the preference ladder.

As a brand increases its overall bank balance, the consumer's perception of it improves, and the brand moves higher up the preference ladder. Brand bank assets ultimately decide the position of brands on this ladder.

(9) The brand preference ladder is dynamic and is updated on every retrieval.

Brands are either consistently upgrading themselves, thus crediting their accounts, or not doing anything and allowing competing brands to debit their accounts. In other words, bank balances are constantly changing, and brands are continuously being repositioned on the preference ladder.

Every time a consumer needs to evaluate a brand, she retrieves her preference ladder and immediately updates it based on new information. As we do not know when a consumer will need to compare brands, brands have to ensure that they are always ahead in the game. Unfortunately, this is a stressful strategy because the brand is then in constant battle with other brands. This brings us to the next principle of brand banking which shows how brands can break out of this cycle.

(10) Brands can avoid this constant struggle by achieving Wowability.

When a contact point turns into a Wow point, Wowability is achieved and the brand acquires an advantage. Clearly the more Wow points a brand has, the better. How to turn contact points into Wow points is a key question and will be addressed in Chapters 8 and 9.

(11) A regular brand bank account is turned into a premium brand bank account when contact points are turned into Wow points.

Satisfying your customers and delivering exactly what the brand promises will increase the brand's bank account balance. But in a world where all brands are vigorously trying to increase their account balances, this is simply not enough. The brand needs to delight its customers by turning its contact points into Wow points.

Examples include Wal-Mart's prices, Ferrari's exclusivity, and the customer experience at Starbucks. These Wow points represent the competitive advantages of these brands, and give them Wowability status as their accounts for price, exclusivity, and customer experience turn into premium accounts.

(12) Brands with premium accounts are always on the top rung of the brand preference ladder, followed by the brand with the highest regular bank account balance.

On the preference ladder, brand banks with premium accounts occupy the highest rungs, while those with regular accounts occupy the lower rungs. Regular brand banks that increase brand equity by either improving existing contact points or by adding new contact points can move up the preference ladder, but will still be below the brand with a premium account. No matter how hard they try, brands with regular contact points can never overtake those with Wow points.

To further improve their position, brands must turn their contact points into Wow points. This is similar to the Olympic Games medal tally: A country with 10 silver medals but no gold medals will still be ranked below a country with a single gold medal.

An example of this can be seen in the mobile phone industry. Nokia leads due to its Wow points in design, product features, and user friendliness, among other things. Other brands, like LG for example, would find it hard to compete with Nokia simply by improving on their contact points, but without turning them into Wow points. If LG can turn some of its contact points into Wow points, by creating a mobile phone with an amazing design, or incorporating features that other mobile phone manufacturers have not thought of, while maintaining its attractive price, it could move up the brand preference ladder to rival Nokia.

Now, this is easier said than done because it means that LG will have to come up with a design that beats not only Nokia, but Samsung and Motorola as well. However, to become the preferred brand, a brand needs to beat the rest. Brands can improve their position by targeting one contact point at a time, accumulating one Wow point at a time.

Conclusion

Brand banking gives a workable approach to understanding how branding works and how to improve a brand's position in the consumer's mind. It shows that for brands to climb the preference ladder and to escape the constant battle to stay ahead, they need Wowability.

Samsung's Wow Story

Samsung has moved out from under the shadow of other major electronics manufacturers to become a brand to contend with. In this way, it has emulated other Asian brands in their journey from obscurity to familiarity, and on to Wowability.

In the current climate of cutthroat competition, it is necessary for a brand to have a strong unified brand message, and to communicate that message effectively to consumers. In this respect, Samsung has exceeded all expectations. The Korean company has also focused on quality and design, and this has clearly worked. It was 20th on Interbrand's best brand rankings in 2005 and 2006, one of only a handful of Asian brands to make the cut.[8] The Samsung master brand bank now stands for something very different from its previous identity as a manufacturer of low-end, mass market products.

Samsung has added to the brand bank accounts of individual products, simultaneously strengthening the master brand bank. It also uses a number of communicational contact points, most notably sports sponsorship, to make the brand better known to consumers. Since 1997, it has been a worldwide partner of the Olympic Games and is committed to continuing this relationship at least until 2016.[9] Its sponsorship deal with Barclay's Premiership champion Chelsea Football Club is the second-largest in its history,[10] and it also owns Suwon Samsung Bluewings, a soccer team in South Korea.[11] These sponsorships create a high degree of familiarity with the brand and add value.

Having a strong master brand is advantageous as the halo effect duplicates some of this perceived positive value and transfers it to the brands under it. However, Samsung has not depended solely on the attractiveness of its master brand. It has focused on creating Wowability on several other fronts to sustain increasing levels of revenue. In the fourth quarter of 2006, Samsung announced revenues of 15.69 trillion won (US$16.6 billion), an increase of 3% over the previous quarter.[12]

As noted earlier, the company has been focusing on improving and creating Wowability in quality and design with much success. To turn design into a Wow point, Samsung almost tripled its global design staff from 2001 to 2005[13] and took calculated moves like relocating from sleepy Suwon to vibrant Seoul[14] in order to attract younger designers. It has a usability laboratory where engineers can study from behind a two-way mirror how consumers interact with the company's products.[15] Samsung also sends its designers to different parts of the world to visit museums and icons of modern architecture, even arranging for some of them to spend a few months at fashion houses, design consultancies, and cosmetics specialists to be inspired by and stay current with trends in other industries.[16] These moves have resulted in unique design features and created value that far exceed the expectations of consumers. They have turned design into a Wow point for Samsung, converting its regular brand bank account into a premium account.

A variety of tactics has also improved quality. The company's Quality College provides regular training programs and certification to its management and workforce.[17] Samsung also frequently conducts reliability tests and quality checks. As a result of these and other such measures, the company has attained a number of quality awards for its products.[18] Quality has become another Wow point for the brand, and the corresponding bank account has thus been upgraded to a premium account.

Samsung places a strong emphasis on innovation to add to its functional value. The Value Innovation Program (VIP) Center is Samsung's intensive camp, where employees from various parts of the company brainstorm ways to add value to the products being developed.[19] Because the participants come from diverse backgrounds, they contribute a wide range of ideas. The results of Samsung's Wowability can be seen in its steady rise up Interbrand's rankings over the years. Samsung has gone from a relatively humble 42nd position in 2001 to 25th place in 2003 and 20th position in 2006.[20]

!

"Practice should
always be based upon
a sound knowledge
of theory."[1]

- Leonardo Da Vinci

chapter ❸

Wowability is the Ability to Consistently Delight by Exceeding Expectations

So what are expectations?

For the purpose of this book, expectations refer to the value that consumers believe they will derive from the brand. Consumers subconsciously assign a value to every contact point that a brand has, and the sum of these values is the overall expectation that consumers have. It is not possible to take into account every contact point that exists for a brand and calculate overall expectations. What we can do is aim to exceed consumer expectations in key contact points and convert these into Wow points.

We need to recognize that in the consumer's mind, there are two categories of value, functional value and emotional value. It is important to recognize the difference between the two because they increase or decrease over time in different ways.

Functional Value

Functional value refers to the perceived benefits that a consumer derives from using a product. This could be the grip of Nike's rock-climbing shoes, the fuel efficiency of Toyota's Prius, or the quality of Starbucks' coffee beans. The functional value of a product is generally taken to be stable as the brand will continue to provide the consumer with the same functional benefits over the years. Functional value over time, thus, looks like this:

Figure 3.1: Functional value over time

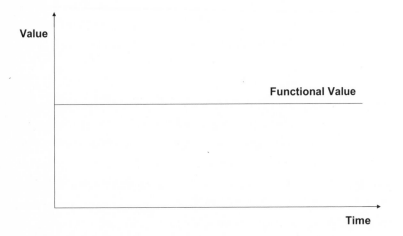

This may not be the case in some product classes, like electronics, for example, given the industry's propensity to keep coming up with new technologies. An electronic product's relative functional value starts going down the moment it is bought. In some cases, it can become obsolete the moment the industry releases a more advanced version. When MP3 players were introduced to the market, many owners of the Mini disc would certainly have felt that, all things being equal, they would rather have had an MP3 player. A graphic representation of the functional value of such a product would look like this:

Figure 3.2: Functional value of an electronic product over time

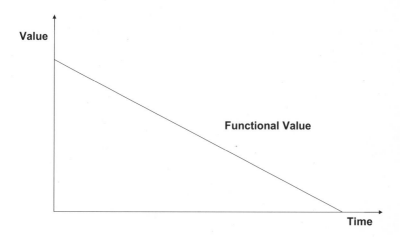

Emotional Value

Emotional value refers to the intangible benefits that consumers derive from acquiring and using a particular product. Whereas functional value comes from the product itself, emotional value mainly derives from what the brand stands for, and from the marketing efforts that position the brand. It comes in the form of prestige, novelty value, uniqueness, exclusivity, and other such characteristics that consumers may attach.

Emotional value, like consumer behavior, is less predictable. For products that are entirely functional in nature, the emotional value that consumers attach to them may be nearly zero, and is unlikely to change over time. This is true of commodities like rice and wheat.

Emotional value can also fall. This could happen when the emotional value attached to a brand is the result of its novelty. Over time, as the product becomes more common and the brand does little to refresh itself, the novelty factor fades and emotional value falls. A graphic representation of such a scenario would look like this:

Figure 3.3: Emotional value when the novelty factor is lost

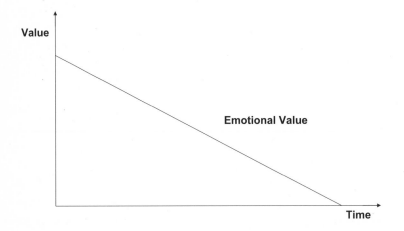

Conversely, the emotional value of a brand could also rise. This could happen if it consistently renewed itself or if its customers developed a sense of loyalty toward it. Harley-Davidson Motor Company, for example, clearly enjoys tremendous customer loyalty, and its emotional value has risen over the years. A graphic representation of emotional value in such a scenario would look like this:

Figure 3.4: Emotional value with consumer loyalty

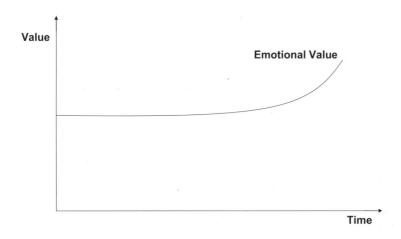

Its customers feel proud to own a Harley-Davidson motorcycle, and many of them belong to the Harley Owners Group (H.O.G.). Among the more prominent activities that H.O.G. members engage in are mass events that feature members riding their Harleys through various towns and cities. H.O.G. membership also offers special privileges. Members can go to Harley-Davidson stores in 41 locations around the U.S., Canada, Europe, and Australia, and pick up a motorcycle to tour the city.[2] This serves as a great promotional tool for the company and gives the Harley-Davidson brand immense emotional value. The Harley-Davidson is seen not only as a motorcycle but also as a lifestyle choice and a ticket into an exclusive group.

To achieve Wowability, a brand needs to exceed the expectations consumers have of its emotional and/or functional value. To get a clearer picture, let's look at separate examples of having Wowability in emotional and functional value.

Wowability by Focusing on Functional Value

When Toyota first entered the American automobile market in 1957,[3] it had little, if any, credibility. For a long time, it was seen as a company that mostly copied technology and was considered to be nothing but "a fast follower."[4] A fast follower waits for other players to take the risk with new designs and ideas before following suit. Toyota was not seen as a manufacturer at the cutting edge of technology, nor was its Japanese heritage seen as an advantage. And so, the expected value of Toyota was rather low to begin with.

The first Toyota cars to be imported and sold in the U.S. market—Toyopet Crown and Tiara—were not successful. In fact, Toyopet Crown had to be withdrawn from the market within two years, having proved unsuitable for long-distance highway driving conditions.[5] Following the unsuccessful launches of these two models, Toyota decided to design a car especially for the U.S. market. This strategy later created the Camry, which remains one of the country's top-selling cars.[6] Today, Toyota's success in the U.S. is attributed to the quality and durability, easy operation, and the user-friendly features of its cars and trucks.[7] Analysts believe the Japanese automaker is poised to overtake General Motors (GM) as the world's biggest automaker in terms of global sales and production, a title GM has held for more than half a century.[8] Toyota's success lies in its ability to exceed consumer expectations in functional contact points like performance, gas mileage, and the comfort of its vehicles.

The Japanese automaker continues to adapt to changing consumer trends. In the mid 1990s, it developed the hybrid Prius that improved fuel efficiency by 50%,[9] a much-needed functional feature against a backdrop of rising fuel costs and environmental concern. This increased the functional value of the Prius beyond what consumers had expected of a Toyota. Since then, Toyota has continued to play up its strengths and has established technological know-how as its competitive advantage. In 2006, Toyota was ranked by Interbrand as the seventh most valuable brand in the world.[10]

Wowability by Focusing on Emotional Value

In the early 1990s, Nokia determined that the cell phone had the potential to become a fashion accessory.[11] Design appeals to the emotions, and Nokia believed that investing in design would pay off.[12] It did. Consumers had become accustomed to the generic black rectangular cell phones of the time when Nokia introduced a line of cool phones that had much more emotional value than the competition. In 1994, Nokia wowed cell phone users worldwide when it launched the Nokia 2100 series, the first cell phone with changeable color covers.[13] As a result, the cell phone became a statement of personal style, communicating the owner's identity more than any other electronic device had done before. Nokia was able to exceed expectations and achieved great success through the emotional value of its products. Nokia also created emotional appeal through features like "e-motions,"[14] a platform that let users send creative images, like a picture of a heart.

When a product has Wowability, consumer expectations of it rise accordingly. However, if the brand's total value does not rise in tandem with these expectations, there will be a point where the two lines will meet, which is where expectations are equivalent to total value. This is the "point of mediocrity," because at this point, the brand is no longer exceeding expectations.

When consumer expectations exceed the brand's total value, consumers are disappointed. Expectations begin to fall, and the brand's reputation suffers. Yet, expectations do not fall overnight because brands with Wowability have premium brand bank accounts, and it takes time for these accounts to be depleted. A brand can attempt to regain Wowability by introducing new product lines with novel and innovative features, for example. Over time, however, consumer expectations of the brand will continue to rise, and if the brand cannot keep up, then consumers will become disappointed. The brand could eventually lose its Wowability.

Wowability Zone

Figure 3.5: Wowability zone

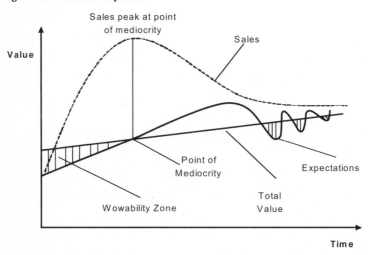

A Wowability Factors Survey my colleagues and I conducted at ADK found an average correlation of 0.90 between Preference and Exceeding Expectations, with 1.00 being perfect correlation. A brand that exceeds expectations is one that is preferred over others.

Figure 3.6: Exceeding Expectations vs. Preference

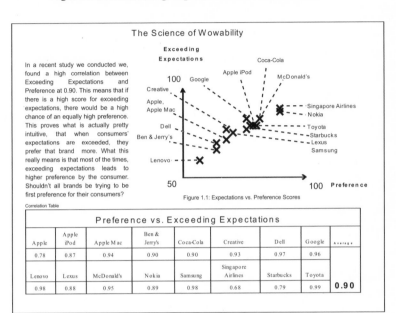

The Science of Wowability

In a recent study we conducted we, found a high correlation between Exceeding Expectations and Preference at 0.90. This means that if there is a high score for exceeding expectations, there would be a high chance of an equally high preference. This proves what is actually pretty intuitive, that when consumers' expectations are exceeded, they prefer that brand more. What this really means is that most of the times, exceeding expectations leads to higher preference by the consumer. Shouldn't all brands be trying to be first preference for their consumers?

Figure 1.1: Expectations vs. Preference Scores

Correlation Table

					Preference vs. Exceeding Expectations			
Apple	Apple iPod	Apple Mac	Ben & Jerry's	Coca-Cola	Creative	Dell	Google	Average
0.78	0.87	0.94	0.90	0.90	0.93	0.97	0.96	
Lenovo	Lexus	McDonald's	Nokia	Samsung	Singapore Airlines	Starbucks	Toyota	
0.98	0.88	0.95	0.89	0.98	0.68	0.79	0.99	**0.90**

Sustaining Wowability

A brand can become a victim of its own success, since consumer expectations grow along with the total value provided. This problem is like trying to walk up an escalator that's moving downwards. In a competitive global market where technology is easily replicated, staying ahead is substantially more difficult than getting there in the first place, and many brands cannot sustain Wowability. These brands are usually unable to increase total value beyond increased expectations. The initial Wowability zone is much smaller than the eventual mediocrity zone. Because the point of mediocrity is reached very early, sales start to fall after an initial spike.

Figure 3.7: A mediocre brand in a competitive market

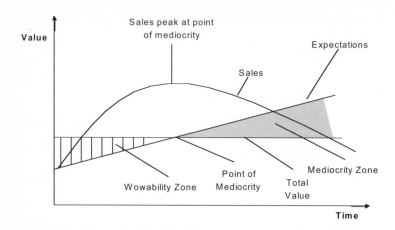

Once a brand reaches a state where expectations exceed total value, the brand has more and more trouble increasing total value to regain Wowability. In a market that is extremely competitive, consumer expectations are unlikely to decline to match total value because competitor brands continue to innovate. As competitors become more innovative, the brand that does not increase its total value quickly becomes outdated. Wowability is not a one-time goal but rather a continuous process.

The Big Picture—Wowability is An Attitude, Not Just a Theory

Brands with Wowability operate very differently from brands without it. Let's go back to the Samsung example. Take a walk inside its VIP (Value Innovation Program) House in Suwon,

South Korea, and you will see dormitories where Samsung engineers, product managers, and researchers forgo sleep to meet project deadlines.[15] Samsung's CEO Jong-Yong Yun warns of the dangers of complacency, and says that difficulties are always present and complications always close at hand. This motivates employees to test their limits.[16] They are intensely proud to be part of the Samsung culture, and gladly put in the time and effort necessary to propel the brand to leadership in the markets where it operates.

When over-dependence on semiconductor chips nearly pushed Samsung into bankruptcy during the 1997 Asian financial crisis, the company drove relentlessly into consumer electronics, striving to achieve and maintain leadership in each of the sectors in which it competes. By keeping ahead of emerging trends in the fast-changing electronics industry and getting employees to share the brand's vision, Samsung has emerged as a global leader in flash memory chips, computer monitors, LCD screens, and CDMA mobile phones.[17]

In the race for market share, a brand first has to run faster than the competition, and once it reaches the head of the pack, it has to maintain its pace to prevent competitors from catching up. In this race, there is no finish line, and there are no clear paths to follow. Competitors behind the leader can easily follow it, merely concentrating on increasing their pace, but the leader has to ensure that its competitors do not catch up even as it takes care not to run into dead ends. These conditions show how hard it is for market leaders to stay ahead. They need to keep abreast of current trends, or they risk missing out on growth opportunities.

Apple's Wow Story

Apple computers and laptops, its iMacs and PowerBooks, are known for their durability and strength. Users report that they are not damaged even when dropped. The PowerBook's casing is enforced with Kevlar, a material used to manufacture bulletproof vests.[18] This definitely exceeds consumer expectations and increases the functional value of the brand. The current Apple operating system is also less prone to crashing, addressing a common frustration that Windows users have faced many times.[19] These advantages are in addition to a faster processing speed and a platform favored by many artists and designers, both of which also add to the functional value of the brand.

The iPod, meanwhile, has raised the bar for MP3 players. Besides the usual specifications of being able to play music and having a reliable compression system and an equalizer, it boasts the click wheel or scroll wheel, a revolutionary new design feature not found on other players before the iPod was launched.[20] The click wheel allows much faster browsing of music. The cool design of the iPod also adds tremendous emotional value to the brand, pushing it higher on the preference ladder. This is clearly demonstrated by iPod's marketshare. In the U.S., iPod controls over 90% of the hard drive-based MP3 player industry.[21] Even when looking at the broader industry of music players, iPod has an impressive 70% share[22] of the market.

Positive consumer response to the iPod has in turn boosted the Apple brand. Additionally, the halo effect has increased overall sales of Apple branded products.

Figure 3.8: Apple Sales[23]

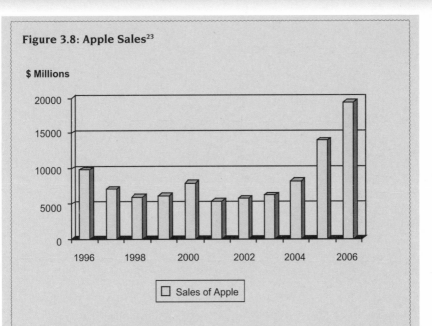

$ Millions

Sales of Apple

The iPod has given Apple Wowability. The first iPod was launched in 2001, and Apple's overall revenue since then has been increasing.[24] Apple is aware that it has to continuously exceed expectations, despite the fact that its own products set these expectations to begin with. Its first-generation iPods were only Mac compatible, but the iPods of the second generation onwards have been Windows compatible as well.[25] The newest models have bigger storage, in addition to being lighter and smaller than their predecessors. In 2004, the iPod Photo was introduced and soon after that, iPods could also play videos. Apple subsequently added PDA-like functions to the iPod and in June 2007, released the iPhone in the U.S.[26] The iPhone is a hand phone that operates in sync with a personal computer. Information, such as music, photos, emails, and personal calendars can be easily uploaded onto the iPhone using a platform similar to that of the iPod.[27] All this exceeds consumer expectations and helps Apple maintain its Wowability.

!

"A brand is a living entity—and it is enriched or undermined cumulatively over time, the product of a thousand small gestures."[1]

– Michael Eisner, CEO, Disney

chapter **4**

Contact points refer to all experiences through which consumers directly or indirectly come into contact with, or obtain information about a brand.

Contact points encompass all points, direct and indirect, through which the consumer obtains information about, or comes into contact with the brand. Whereas touch-points and contact points both include advertising, customer service, and brochures, contact points also include things like product design, the impression that consumers have of the company's leadership, word-of-mouth advertising, and the brand's involvement in community service. Intangible aspects like the charisma of Steve Jobs, co-founder and CEO of Apple, and media, like internet blogs and podcasts, all provide information about various brands and are powerful contact points. One of the key differences between contact points and touch-points is that while touch-points mostly refer solely to things over which the company has direct control, contact points include things over which the company may not have any direct control.

Every brand has hundreds of contact points, and consumers attach varying degrees of importance and expectations to them. For example, mattress softness may be the most important contact point when a consumer is looking for a bed, while the color of the head post may be the contact point with the least importance. Consumers may attach different degrees of importance to the same contact point in different brands. For example, while consumers may see customer service as being extremely important for Starbucks, it is not a priority when thinking about Coca-Cola. Even in the same industry, we all know of supermarkets where we shop for the cheapest prices. Do we really consider customer service as important there as at higher-priced supermarkets?

Brands also need to consider that consumers are more aware of the contact points that are important to them. Psychologists call this phenomenon selective attention.[2] A person interested in technical details would probably show a spike in attentiveness when reading a car advertisement about a new model with twice the engine capacity of the previous one. On the other hand, advertisements featuring new designs and colors may capture the attention of someone who is more aesthetically inclined.

Knowledge of the relative importance of contact points is vital to a brand trying to formulate strategies for Wowability. This will allow the brand to direct its resources toward the more important contact points, while educating consumers on why a seemingly less important one should be given more attention. Ultimately, the positioning of a brand depends on the contact points it chooses to focus on.

Positioning

Consider the positioning of Wal-Mart: a wide variety of products, low prices, efficient service, and strategic locations in the suburban U.S.[3] These Wow points were not randomly chosen, but rather, are contact points valued by the consumer and effectively provided by the company.

Louis Vuitton, on the other hand, is marketed as a luxury brand, and emphasizes quality, design, and exclusivity. Its distinctive style makes LV bags easily distinguishable from other luxury handbags. A low price tag is obviously not a factor that Louis Vuitton chooses to pursue, and contact points like advertising and functionality receive less attention. Louis Vuitton focuses on the contact points that are important to its target market and, like Wal-Mart, has paid less attention to other contact points. This has positioned Louis Vuitton very strongly in the minds of its consumers, a strategy repaid with customer loyalty and word-of-mouth support.

Apple defied convention in the way it launched the iPod into the market. Instead of focusing on its functional aspects and promoting sound quality, long battery life, and performance, the brand positioned itself as the one offering the best user experience. Its advertisements[4] portrayed none of its functional aspects, except that it played music, showing instead the great delight of iPod users in their sleek, new gadget. The clean lines of its design contributed to the coolness of the iPod, and its features quickly created multiple Wow points in the easy-to-use arena.

From the perspective of the brand, the relative importance of contact points can be calibrated into different strategies to position the brand on the market. Wal-Mart, Louis Vuitton, and iPod focus on the key contact points relevant to their target markets. Taking a contact point approach is a great help to a brand that is trying to improve its positioning while creating Wow points allows the brand to maintain first-preference status in the minds of consumers.

Even across brands in the same industry, there are differences in the relative importance placed on contact points as a result of positioning. Without positioning, the relative importance placed on the different contact points is likely to be similar. For a consumer considering a car purchase, the important contact points might be safety, performance, value, and prestige. But do all brands emphasize these equally? What about a Chinese car brand trying to penetrate a super-competitive developed market? In May 2007, a team of 10 MBA students from Singapore's S.P. Jain Business School conducted a study involving face-to-face interviews with 100 Singapore residents. Their goal was to extrapolate the contact points that Chinese auto manufacturer Chery should focus on to effectively penetrate the Singapore market. They found price, value in terms of power and fuel efficiency, and interior design to be of key importance. Using this information, they were able to propose actionable strategies that Chery could use to upgrade these contact points into Wow points. Car brands have generally tried to distinguish themselves from each other by creating strong associations with certain contact points. Volvo distinguishes itself by emphasizing safety, whereas BMW stands for performance. Toyota, meanwhile, equates itself with value, and Mercedes emphasizes prestige. Even within the same industry, it can be strikingly clear how a brand is positioned just by looking at the contact points it has chosen to focus on.

Picking Your Battles

Brands literally have hundreds of contact points, and no company could excel in every one. Consumers themselves are unlikely to be aware of all the brand's contact points. And so, for practical reasons, brands should figure out the best contact points to concentrate on. These should be the ones that are important to, or have the potential to become important to consumers, and the ones where the company can realistically excel.

Focusing on a small number of contact points makes it easier for consumers to understand the positioning of the brand, which is a great advantage in itself. Clear, strong, and relevant positioning can be a brand's strongest asset. Another advantage a clear focus offers is that it gets all the brand's stakeholders on the same page. Knowing where the focus of the company lies gives employees a sense that the additional effort necessary to achieve Wowability is manageable and will not add too much pressure to the existing system. At the same time, the management's focus on select contact points sends a clear message to employees that these contact points are really important and will be closely monitored. This puts additional momentum behind creating Wow points.

Classification of Contact Points

Every contact point can yield both emotional and functional value to varying degrees. The classification of a contact point is based on the degree of emotional and functional value the consumer feels. For example, price might be an emotional contact point in the case of a premium or very low cost brand, but would be a functional contact point where different brands are similarly priced. There are three main categories of contact points: functional, emotional, and communicational.

Functional contact points relate directly to the utilitarian and quantitative aspects of a product or service. These contact points are usually the functional attributes of the brand. They may have some emotional value, but they largely give functional value.

For products, functional aspects may include the engine capacity of cars, the screen size of high-definition TVs, or the mineral content of mineral water. For services, they may include interest rates, the quality of stocks recommended, the timeliness of service or even the length of queues at the cashier.

The value that comes from most functional contact points often comes down to technological superiority or operational excellence. Besides improving on these, the brand could also innovate to add additional functional value that may be prized by consumers. Coming back to the Chery example, one of the team's recommendations was to hire local designers to upgrade the interiors of the cars. The idea was to transform this tangible contact point into a Wow point, which would then be communicated to consumers by the brand's salespeople. Once consumers began to associate Chery with excellent interiors, the brand could then develop a positioning beyond its low-cost advantage. When a brand decides that it wants to increase its functional value, it targets its key functional contact points. Since the value of functional contact points is driven by technology and processes, brands can divert resources for innovation and improvements to these areas.

Emotional contact points invoke some degree of emotional attachment to the brand. These include customer service, design, country of origin, the brand story, and brand leadership, among others.

The best way to increase emotional value is less clear. However, emotional value may be relatively less costly to increase than functional value. Brand owners need to understand the brand experience from the consumer's point of view to look for opportunities to increase emotional value. It is only with the creation of emotional bonds that emotional value will rise.

The brand must come up with Wow points that create and strengthen the emotional bond with its customers. An example of a company that has successfully done this is Build-A-Bear Workshop. Located in more than 19 countries,[5] it offers a customer base—ranging from small children to adults—the opportunity to create a personalized bear. Customers can choose from more than 30 different styles, which they stuff,[6] dress, shoe, and accessorize. The process of building a teddy bear includes placing a small heart and a wish inside it. This creates an emotional connection for the person making the teddy bear.[7] What is also unique about these bear-making stores is that each bear is entered into the Build-a-Bear database and given a personalized birth certificate.[8] The process of entering one's bear into the database gives life to the stuffed animal, which in turn makes customers, particularly children, feel more attached to their own special bears. Build-A-Bear is successful because it has gone beyond your typical teddy bear retail store and turned its emotional contact points into Wow points. Thinking of ways to increase emotional value is difficult, but there are major gains to be had. The primary one is that once emotional bonds are formed, they are enduring and difficult for competitors to replicate. Functional improvements are easier to replicate than emotional value.

Communicational contact points encompass all forms of company and consumer communications. These include advertising, blogging, forums, and word-of-mouth. Communications can be functional or emotional depending on the message and the medium used. Value, whether functional or emotional, is largely dependent on the perception of the consumer. The role of communicational contact points, then, is to shape the consumer's perception of the brand. Communicational contact points work at three levels: at the cognitive level, by increasing awareness of and familiarity with the brand; at the affective level, by changing consumer attitudes towards the brand; and at the behavioral level, by increasing sales and store visits. There is little to be gained if the brand has made a large investment to increase its value but then does not convey this to consumers. The communicational contact point here plays a functional role and increases the functional value of the brand as well. In other cases, communicational contact points evoke a desire to use the brand. They also associate the brand with certain characteristics. These serve to increase the emotional value of the brand.

Starbucks' Wow Story

What makes Starbucks unique is that it has consciously attained Wowability in contact points across several categories. It has been able to increase both its functional and emotional value through fortifying its functional, emotional, and communicational contact points. Today, the coffee chain enjoys increasing revenues and a growing number of outlets across the globe. Starbucks is still in its Wowability zone. But how did the U.S. coffee chain get there in the first place?

To begin with, it has never compromised on the resources necessary to improve its functional contact points, primarily the most obvious one—the quality of its coffee. Every coffee company should by right ensure the highest possible quality of coffee, but in 1971,[9] when Starbucks first started out, this was not the case.

The worldwide chain began life as a coffee store. Its three founding fathers roasted and sold whole coffee beans for home consumption, positioning Starbucks as the source of quality coffee. They also educated consumers on how great coffee should taste. The standard of coffee provided by Starbucks far exceeded the expectations of customers, creating functional value for the brand that was much higher than that of other coffee brands, and turned the quality of its coffee into a Wow point. When Howard Schultz took over in 1982, Starbucks had broadened into other beverages but kept its focus on providing quality coffee, thus keeping its grip on this Wow point.

> **Apply the highest standards of excellence to the purchasing, roasting and fresh delivery of our coffee.**
> Starbucks Mission Statement[10]

Sustaining "quality of coffee" as a Wow point requires Starbucks' involvement in the entire production chain, from securing quality coffee beans to brewing the perfect cup. Its senior vice president, Dave Olsen, frequently visits coffee-growing regions, personally checking on the crops and yields, and improving Starbucks' relationship with its growers. This ensures consistently high-quality coffee beans.[11] The company only buys Arabica coffee, as opposed to the lower quality Robusta coffee, willingly paying the premium it commands.[12]

Having high-quality green coffee beans would not result in an aromatic, full-bodied cup of coffee if the roasting process was poor. Starbucks has its roots in coffee roasting and continues to roast its own coffee. Highly trained and experienced roasters keep a sharp eye on this process, and Olsen himself, when he is not traveling, samples the coffee and records his observations.[13] Over time, however, consumers have come to expect this level of quality control from Starbucks. It is also no longer unique in this respect. Many of these measures have been implemented by other premium coffee brands. Starbucks, however, has gone a step further, testing coffee bean batches using a 'blood cell analyzer,' and discarding entire batches that do not meet prescribed quality standards.[14]

Ground-roasted coffee is ready to be brewed, and baristas are trained in making the perfect cup. Starbucks' baristas must fulfill a minimum of 24 hours of training, which includes, among other things, how to pull the right espresso shot in 18 to 23 seconds.[15] The 18-to -23-second rule ensures that the espresso is strong but not bitter. Baristas are also trained in making the chain's other coffee-based drinks, such as Caramel Macchiato and the various coffee Frappuccinos.[16] These efforts are needed to bring the perfect cup of coffee to the table.

Starbucks understands the power of a strong brand in connecting with customers, and Schultz admits that it was always the company's intention to "build an emotional connection with (our) customers."[17] Starbucks has actively sought not only to add to its functional value but also to increase its emotional value with exceptional customer service. In addition, it strives to strengthen another contact point, location, by opening as many outlets as possible, thus ensuring easy access. The focus on these two contact points complements another facet of Starbucks' overall positioning strategy, which is to create a "third place."[18] This is a place, other than work or home, where people can go to relax and meet friends. It must be comfortable enough that a customer develops an affinity for it, and be conveniently located.

Starbucks' baristas represent the depth of the relationship that customers have with the brand. Removing baristas from the picture, a cup of coffee at Starbucks would simply be expensive gourmet coffee.

Beyond being efficient and polite, Starbucks' baristas build friendships with customers. According to Shultz, "our people have done a wonderful job of knowing your drink, your name, your kids' names and what you do for a living."[19] This practice goes beyond mere customer service and adds tremendous emotional value to the Starbucks brand.

The Wow point of customer service (though the term fails to do justice to the relationships established) is difficult to monitor. While the quality of coffee can be measured, one cannot quantify the level of friendliness of a barista. Starbucks has succeeded in maintaining this quality in its baristas by propagating a culture of respect, providing a positive work environment, and investing heavily in them.[20] In the U.S., Starbucks employees are called "partners" and any partner that works 20 hours a week or more is entitled to health benefits.[21] This motivates employees to stay with the company. Starbucks also tries to build a relationship of trust with its employees by showing them that their input is valued: at Starbucks, constructive criticism is rewarded, and some of the best ideas have percolated up from the front line staff.[22] The company understands that because retailers and restaurants rely heavily on customer service, they must invest in their people. Schultz insists, not without grounds, that the sporadic nature of investments made by restaurants and retailers in their people is the reason that "retail experiences are mediocre for the public."[23]

Starbucks' primary emotional contact point remains its people, who continuously increase the brand's emotional value by building relationships with customers. It ensures that the contact point is turned into a Wow point by treating its "partners" well. As Schultz so eloquently said, "You can't expect your employees to exceed the expectations of your customers if you don't exceed the employees' expectations of management."[24]

One factor that makes Starbucks unlike other brands on Interbrand's 100 Best Brands list is that it does not advertise:[25] The company has chosen to use other communicational contact points to add value to its brand. Instead of advertising, it has implemented a culture and value system for its employees[26] that create a great customer service experience. Customers are then happy to recommend Starbucks to their families and friends. Word-of-mouth would not be favorable if other contact points disappointed the customer. But Starbucks is confident in its strategy, and the results so far have shown that it works. For loyal Starbucks customers, a glimpse of the green and white logo is enough to excite and attract them. They are also very enthusiastic about bringing others to share in the Starbucks experience.

Although Starbucks has certainly succeeded in transforming many contact points into Wow points, it has chosen to pay less attention to other contact points. The most criticized of these is price.[27] It certainly does not offer the cheapest cup of coffee, but it has never intended to do so. It is positioned to offer great coffee and has never compromised on that.

Starbucks has come a long way from its modest beginnings in Seattle.[28] The steady growth it has enjoyed and its dedication to maintaining Wowability suggests that the company is likely to grow much further.

!

"A fundamental rule in technology says that whatever can be done will be done."[1]

– Andrew Grove, Co-Founder, Intel

chapter **5**

The Wowability Factors Survey, which my ADK colleagues and I undertook in the summer of 2006, demonstrates the correlation between Functional Value and Exceeding Expectations. Our findings showed an average correlation of 0.78 between the two factors, but figures for brands like Ben & Jerry's and Coca-Cola were substantially higher. In these cases, the brands have effectively used functional contact points like product variety and taste to exceed consumer expectations and achieve Wowability. More details on the study and methodology employed can be found in Appendix I.

Figure 5.1: Exceeding Expectations vs. Functional value

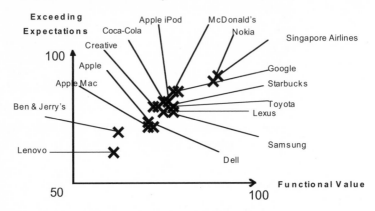

Figure 5.1: Expectations vs. Functional Value Scores

Apple	Apple iPod	Apple Mac	Ben & Jerry's	Coca-Cola	Creative	Dell	Google	Average
0.75	0.83	0.85	0.93	0.90	0.83	0.74	0.79	
Lenovo	Lexus	McDonald's	Nokia	Samsung	Singapore Airlines	Starbucks	Toyota	
0.79	0.48	0.92	0.84	0.78	0.74	0.80	0.56	**0.78**

One of the most quantifiable methods to increase functional value would be to increase the technological sophistication of the product through research and development efforts or innovation. But raising the level of technology may not necessarily add enough value to the contact point to turn it into a Wow point. Consumers may see the increase in functional value, but improved perceptions may not reflect the amount of investment poured into a functional contact point. Also, in today's fast-paced world, technology is easily replicated. And so, while functional value is essential for any product to remain relevant, a brand must also tap into other categories of contact points to get a stronger grip on its Wowability. Having said that, functional contact points are extremely important. Without some of them, a product would have little reason to exist.

Features

There are two main ways for a brand to achieve Wowability in its features. It can exceed expectations by upgrading existing features or by increasing the number of features that its products have.

Brands that are well established and have won strong customer loyalty usually upgrade existing features to maintain their edge in the market. This strategy relies on technological know-how. To constantly improve on this technological capability, the brand needs to make huge investments in research and development. BMW is one company that does this. In order to ensure that its products sport the most technologically advanced features, the company built an information technology research centre in the U.S. in 2005.[2] One of the centre's recent discoveries led to an improvement in BMW's fuel efficiency and a reduction in emissions. Another enhancement to the BMW car series has been the addition of a display windshield where information, such as vehicle speed, navigation directions, and the distance to be maintained from the vehicle ahead are shown.[3] While not earth shattering, these innovations still represent improvements on pre-existing features, and are aimed at exceeding consumer expectations. Ultimately, this strategy relies on the technological know-how of the brand. To improve its technology, the brand will need to make a hefty investment in research and development. Not every company has this option.

Another strategy would be to try to increase the number of features the product offers. This strategy is, arguably, less costly because the brand only has to figure out which features from those available in the company or the market should be paired together, and how. This pairing invariably leads to the loss of simplicity, but if consumers see the net effect as an addition to value and one that exceeds their expectations, then the brand has moved a step closer toward Wowability.

The second strategy is commonly seen in the cell phone industry, although no cell phone brand would entirely forgo the first. The average cell phone today is able to take photos, record videos, organize schedules, double as an alarm, play MP3 files, and even comes with built-in games. Ironically, not only do these features have nothing to do with making phone calls, they may even make the incoming calls seem like a disruption. This multitude of features makes buying a cell phone fairly complicated.

The race to inundate the basic cellular phone with as many features as possible began in earnest in 1997 when the first commercial camera phone built by Philippe Kahn hit the market.[4] Most brands jumped almost immediately onto the bandwagon, and in a relatively short 10-year span, it has become extremely rare to find a phone that does not have a camera function. Instead, brands are competing to give consumers the best picture and video quality. Today, several camera phones on the market boast Carl Zeiss lenses, a trend initiated by Nokia in 2005. These lenses allow cell phone users to take high resolution pictures.[5] But camera functions are hardly the only additional feature in today's mobile phones. Games have become another highly sought-after feature. N-gage, by Nokia, is positioned for the gaming enthusiast and has the capability to engage other gamers over Bluetooth or the internet. Its controls are designed after those on the standard gaming console. Clearly, there has been a high degree of improvement in certain key contact points. Yet the makers didn't stop there; N-gage also has organizer functions based on a Symbian OS. It plays music, and one can watch videos on it. Despite an apparent focus on gaming functions, Nokia still used the conventional strategy to pack N-gage with a multitude of other functions. This race to provide as many applications as possible, on top of a focus on certain contact points, adds a tremendous amount of value for the user and may even create Wowability for the brand owner.

A brand can either improve on existing features or add to them to increase the total functional value of its products. The question as to which method would work best largely depends on the positioning of the brand and its overall strategy. Either way, the brand should not forget that the tactic chosen is only a means of achieving Wowability. Even if it succeeds in compacting many features into a device or making large improvements to existing features, all these efforts will not necessarily translate into Wowability if consumers do not perceive that the moves have increased the total value of the brand.

Quality

Quality holds functional value. The higher the quality of a product, the higher its functional value. Independent bodies exist to evaluate quality, though the system is far from perfect. The ISO 9000 defines quality as the degree to which a set of inherent characteristics fulfils requirements.[6] Standards like the ISO 9000 ensure that brands meet certain benchmarks with regards to performance and the product's composition, among other things. This gives consumers some assurance regarding the .brand, especially if the quality is not easily perceivable or if consumers do not have enough information to judge for themselves. However, the ISO 9000 cannot provide a comparison of quality across brands. It only confirms that a product has met certain minimum requirements.

Quality also has to do with how well the various features function. A number of characteristics would fall into this category. The most pertinent ones are reliability, performance, and durability.

A high quality product must first be reliable. The same switch or button must perform the same function every time it is used. This seems highly intuitive, and most consumers take it for granted. Yet to imagine the power button not switching the computer on would add a new empathetic paradigm to this concept. Consumers may not fully value reliability until the product starts to malfunction. If this happens soon after purchase, consumers will immediately reduce the functional value of the brand. Conversely, if the product is consistently reliable and remains so for longer than expected, consumer expectations are exceeded, and the brand is working its way towards Wowability.

Performance is another aspect that brands need to consider in order to increase product quality. It is no longer enough that the brand has products that are reliable and have the same features as other brands on the market. Its performance must be superior to those of other brands. If the product is a car, then its engine must be able to exceed consumer expectations in terms of horsepower, say, for it to gain any degree of Wowability. Often technology-driven industries flaunt such excellence in available literature to entice consumers to buy their products. It is also common for critics to compare the performance of various contact points across different brands in order to help consumers in the decision-making process. As with other functional contact points, brands improve their performance primarily through research and development, thus increasing their total functional value and allowing them to move toward Wowability.

The third aspect of quality is durability. The more durable the product is, the higher the perceived quality of the brand.

From the consumer's point of view, durable products are definitely a good idea. Although the consumer may not need the product to last a lifetime, knowing that it can last that long adds an amazing amount of value to the brand. Consumers will pay higher prices for quality products, reasoning that the amount spent, spread over a longer period of time, would be relatively lower.

Deuter is a German brand of haversacks that has been around for more than a hundred years[7] and is famous for its design, quality, and innovative features. These outdoors bags can withstand the harshest environments, making them extremely durable[8] and giving the brand a fantastic reputation among mountaineers. Offering a lifetime warranty[9] confirms the brand's positioning as a maker of durable bags.

Because consumers perceive Deuter as a high quality brand, they are willing to pay premium prices for its products. Deuter's durability gives the brand Wowability, which ultimately leads to top-of-mind consideration when purchasing outdoor products, and making repeat purchases.

Another example of a brand known for its superior quality and durability is Rolex. Established in 1905, the brand has maintained this reputation for over a century. In the post-war years, technology standardized the production of watches. Norwegian-born engineer Joakim Lehmkuhl, for instance, devised a dependable and inexpensive way of producing quartz crystal watches that could be mass produced. These watches were marketed under the brand name Timex.[10] Despite the new technologies that were rapidly being introduced, Rolex continued to emphasize craftsmanship and quality. Its products were, and still are, made of gold, platinum, and precious jewels, which greatly increase their value and price. Today, an inexpensive quartz watch is mass manufactured using between

50 and 100 parts, whereas a Rolex is handmade with some 220 parts, emphasizing its time-honored craftsmanship and quality. Rolex's focus on quality creates extremely durable watches that are regularly passed down through the generations.[11]

Since the turn of the 20th century, much attention has been paid to improving the quality of products and manufacturing processes. One of the most significant innovations was the Six Sigma concept popularized by Motorola in the late 1980s and 1990s. Motorola's Bill Smith came up with the concept in 1986[12] as a way to quantify and control product defects, hence enhancing quality. It was so successfully implemented that in the 18 years since its inception, it had reportedly saved Motorola $17 billion.[13] At the most basic level, Six Sigma is a defect reduction tool. It allows a company to analyze its business processes and streamline operations, with exceptional quality as the ultimate goal. Six Sigma has been applied in various fields, including banking, insurance and healthcare.

Convenience

Convenience is another intangible functional contact point. By making products that are convenient to use, companies add to their functional value. Not only can the product perform the functions that it is designed for, but the fact that it's easy to use will make consumers prefer it to other brands. A lot of us still remember the hassle of cleaning hard contact lenses. Disposable contact lenses have come as a great relief. Another classic example is Gillette's disposable razor blades. Its inventor, King Camp Gillette, realized that it was a hassle to re-sharpen razors after they became dull from prolonged use.[14] As long as the cost to acquire these consumables is a reasonable exchange for less hassle, consumers will prefer them to others.

Many consumers saw the benefits of a disposable razor blade, and preferred it to the ones they were using. Similarly, the potential problems from contact lenses that are not cleaned properly prompted many consumers to switch to lenses that are disposed after each use. Disposability is a Wow point because it increases convenience.

Location

Because location is not an attribute that is built into a product, it may receive less attention than contact points, such as features. Nevertheless, location is extremely functional because it allows for the product to be acquired. Even if a strong enough demand for the product is created, the brand would suffer if consumers did not know where to buy it or if they found the location inconvenient.

Product Location and Communications Placement

Product location can be divided into two categories: store location and in-store location. Product location gives functional value simply by making the product easily available to the consumer. Brands like Starbucks, 7-Eleven, and McDonald's have thousands of outlets. These brands put themselves in as many locations as possible to afford consumers convenience and the chance to enjoy their products wherever they are. The more convenient it is to locate these brands, the easier it is for consumers to place these brands in their consideration set. Often, the most important factor in a purchase decision is convenience. This is especially true for basic products. Having numerous outlets allows 7-Eleven to often be the first to be considered when consumers feel thirsty or need a quick snack. The brand has certainly managed to create Wowability in its location contact point by being everywhere. Few competitors can replicate this degree of ubiquity. Consumer expectations on this count were low in the pre-7-Eleven days, allowing the chain to quickly convert its pervasive presence into a Wow point.

Wal-Mart has succeeded where few other discount retailers have been able to, profitably setting up mega-stores in suburban U.S. Having incredible size and clout, the "Behemoth of Bentonville" can provide a wide variety of products at low prices to the residents of these areas. Because the population density in these areas tends to be very low, few competitors are willing to set up a store to compete with Wal-Mart. The prices that the discount retailer charges its suburban customers are much lower than they have been used to paying, and because Wal-Mart is able to be in places that other retailers avoid, it once again exceeds expectations, earning Wowability.

On another level, we see that the location of products within stores plays a big part in their sales. You tend to see the most popular brands placed at eye level or displayed in the most prominent areas of supermarkets. These display areas are priced above less prominent areas because they allow otherwise overlooked products to be seen and picked up by consumers. Because good shelf space is expensive, only successful brands are usually able to afford it.

The location of advertisements and other communicational contact points may also have very high functional value. Location primarily bridges the gap between the communicational contact point and the consumer, allowing the message to come across, regardless of whether it is functional or emotional in nature. The more locations the communicational contact points have, the more the message percolates, strengthening the brand's image and stimulating trial.

Country-of-Origin Effect

The country of origin may have a functional value. For example, chocolates that are produced in Belgium are widely considered better than those produced in other countries because Belgium has an especially long chocolate-making tradition. Thus chocolates that are made in Belgium tend to have a higher functional value than chocolates made elsewhere. In other words, the reputation of a country can have a halo effect on the products produced there.

A 2005 study by Liu and Johnson found that the country of origin affects product evaluation even when participants are instructed not to let it do so.[15] Participants in the study were asked to choose between different notebook brands. Notebooks were chosen because a previous study showed that notebook evaluation involved "extensive attribute-based processing," meaning that notebook purchases typically involved evaluating all the functional attributes of the choices available, and then choosing the product that best fulfilled consumer needs. Attributes deemed important were printed along with the country of origin in eight advertisements that were shown to participants. The two countries selected for the study were Japan and China. Participants, most of whom were Americans, were divided into two groups and were shown the advertisements. They were then asked to evaluate the notebooks based on attributes, and to regard the country of origin fairly because notebooks made in either country had an equal chance of being good. The results showed that despite being told this, participants still relied on stereotypes of each country when making their evaluation and regarded notebooks made in Japan as superior to those made in China.

There are plenty of examples of brands that try to downplay their countries of origin, like the U.S. ice-cream brand Haägen-Dazs. It was launched in 1961 by Reuben Mattus who wanted to create a brand of ice cream that would "convey an aura of the old-world traditions and craftsmanship."[16] The name adds to the perception of the brand as European, and its packaging does not prominently feature its country of origin.

Another example is the Lexus. Toyota's management did not want its "flagship" LS Series to have any obvious link to the Toyota brand mainly because its image in the late 1980s was that of a low-end car manufacturer.[17] There was a lot at stake: Toyota had spent over US$1 billion developing the first Lexus, the LS 400. The luxury car was developed from the ground up, sharing few parts with Toyota. Also, Toyota did not sell Lexus through its existing dealers in the U.S. Rather, it set up new dealerships and showrooms to sell it separately. This strategy was a success. Many Americans thought the car was European. Fortunately, when consumers realized that Lexus was part of the Toyota stable, it did not create a significant backlash for the company. This was mainly because the product was seen as indeed comparable to BMW and Mercedes, and was moreover available at a lower price. Toyota's brand image is now vastly improved, with more prestigious Toyota cars offered alongside the maturing Lexus brand.

If a brand tries to downplay or even conceal its country of origin, there may be ethical issues involved, but that discussion is beyond the scope of this book. Brands like Lenovo, Acer, and Mahindra face an uphill battle convincing consumers that their products are not inferior just because they are manufactured in China, Taiwan, and India, respectively. It bears pointing out that Japanese-made electronic products were once stereotyped as inferior, and American-made electronic products were considered superior to them. Lenovo's purchase of IBM's PC and notebook business was always going to be tough for the mainland China company. It will have to fight the stigma attached to Chinese electronics brands. Meanwhile, its decision to continue to use the IBM logo on the ThinkPad series for the five years following its 2005 acquisition represents a rough timeframe within which it has to convince the public that it can build on the success of the series. With Bill Amelio as CEO of the company, the way Lenovo conducts its global business is certainly not typical of what people expect from a Chinese company. Brands whose country of origin is not in their favor should heed the lessons of Lexus (and Lenovo if it proves to be successful in the future) and seek to disprove the perceptions that consumers have of them. Stereotyping occurs only when information is not available, and only mediocre brands allow stereotyping to work against them. Brands with Wowability overturn stereotypes—Sony of Japan and Samsung of South Korea are good examples—and become trailblazers for other brands in their home countries.

Toyota's Wow Story

When it was suggested that Toyota had become quite successful and could now relax, Fujio Cho, the president of Toyota Motor Corporation likened running the company to "trying to pull a handcart up a steep hill."[18] He said: "There's always a tremendous danger that if we relax, even for a moment, we could lose momentum and be thrown to the bottom."

Brands that have Wowability, like Toyota, understandably want to maintain the advantage that it gives. They understand that they have to constantly improve as consumer expectations rise.

Looking at Toyota however, it is difficult to see the cause for this concern. Since 2000, it has steadily gained market share and is today the world's second-largest automaker, having overtaken Ford in 2003. Analysts predict that if General Motors' downtrend continues, Toyota will become the world's largest automaker.

The Japanese company's reluctance to relax and bask in its success may be due to the fact that this success is still relatively new. Only in the last two decades has the company been able to establish itself as a stable and prosperous brand name. The Lexus division was launched in 1989 while its signature hybrid car, Prius, went on sale in 1997. Since then, it has received much attention from the industry and consumers alike, and has moved significantly up the brand preference ladder.

Toyota has made improvements to almost every aspect of its cars, earning a reputation for incorporating new technologies that add value and exceed existing consumer expectations while establishing new ones. The Prius is an excellent example of this.

Toyota's success in adding to its functional value has been mainly due to a highly efficient manufacturing process called kaizen. This is a philosophy that tries to minimize wastage and yield the greatest efficiency possible.[19] In response to the early 1990s labor crisis in Japan, for instance, Toyota used kaizen to modify its assembly line and wage systems to make them more employee-friendly.

The Toyota Production System (TPS) has been repeatedly used to exemplify kaizen and has allowed Toyota not only to make better quality cars, but also to turn them out faster. At the outset, TPS made use of standardization[20] to ensure that consistent quality was maintained. Every process in the production plant was analyzed, and a target was set to ensure that everyone would work toward continuous improvement. This reduced waste in time, parts, and resources. If there was any slack in the system, the target was reevaluated and subsequently tightened. On the surface, continuous improvement may appear to have only benefited Toyota as it increased the company's profit margin. However, due to operational excellence and the efficiency of the system, much more value was passed on to the consumer without a corresponding increase in costs.

Now the spirit of continuous improvement is ingrained in the Toyota culture. Everyone is responsible for his work and is expected to take the initiative to suggest and make improvements. Although it is difficult to track exactly which changes add more value than others, consumers ultimately recognize that the latest Toyota model is of higher quality than its predecessor. Functional value is thus added to the brand, elevating it on the preference ladder.

Toyota employees are also more in tune with the idea of transferring value to the consumer rather than with the practice of meeting minimum expectations and hiding mistakes. Any employee involved in the production process can stop the production line if he discovers a mistake. As manufacturers, there is a natural tendency not to want to stop production. However, the Toyota way is perhaps more logical as it prevents defects that reduce functional value from being replicated.

Lexus is a separate division created by Toyota in 1989 to disassociate its luxury products from the low-end perception that consumers had of the overall brand at that time. Creating the Lexus involved 24 engineering teams made up of 1,400 engineers and 2,300 technicians, and cost Toyota over US$1 billion.[21] Ironically, when Lexus' parentage was made known, the reputations of both brands actually improved and were elevated by the halo effect. The Toyota brand was number seven on Interbrand's Best Global Brands ranking in 2006, beating Mercedes at number 10, and BMW at number 15.[22]

From the beginning, the engine of the Lexus was a really powerful, yet efficient, machine. Compared to other luxury brands, its top speed was some 7mph higher, and its high-speed fuel consumption, 17% lower. The Lexus was also known for its reliability. Engineers tested the car to make sure that it was able to withstand at least 50,000 miles of driving, a distance equivalent to going twice around the world. Lexus engines were minutely inspected by engineers, sometimes even with stethoscopes, to ensure zero defects and optimum performance.

In 1997,[23] Toyota also successfully created and marketed Prius, the world's first hybrid car. It is an excellent example of how adopting disruptive technologies can be a way to sustain overall brand Wowability.

The birth of the Prius was less than smooth, especially when the prototype refused to start up less than two years before the car was scheduled to go into production. But Toyota firmly believed that higher fuel efficiency would be the driving force behind the industry and would be critical to its future.

Its goal was to achieve better fuel efficiency than traditional internal combustion engines, with a target of 47.5 miles per gallon. This represented a 50% improvement in fuel efficiency compared to the standards of the time. The Prius also had added emotional value because it burned fuel more cleanly than non-hybrids.

Although it was priced at a premium, the long-term benefits that consumers derived through lower fuel consumption and a reduction in pollution more than compensated for this. It did, however, take some time for consumers to warm up to the Prius, primarily because of a degree of skepticism toward hybrid technology.

Once consumers became familiar with the technology, Prius started to sell more steadily. Its popularity among celebrities also endeared the car to the public. Even so, Toyota did not rest on its laurels. Anticipating moves by rival companies to replicate the technology, the Japanese automaker continued to make improvements to the Prius, maintaining its grip on Wowability.

Given this level of commitment, it is no wonder that the U.S. auto industry awarded Lexus and Toyota 11 of 19 Initial Quality Model Awards following its 2007 Initial Quality Study. The awards are an industry benchmark of the quality and design of new vehicles, and are based on the experiences of new car owners.

Toyota plans on adding a diesel as well as a hybrid line of pick up trucks for the North American market in 2009.[24] Consumers see this as adding value to the mother brand and as an indication that Toyota's technology has sufficiently advanced for it to break into a new segment of the automotive industry. This too has pushed the brand up the preference ladder.

Google's Wow Story

Starting in 1998 as a student project in a dorm room at Stanford University,[25] Google has grown to become one of the biggest technology companies in the world. Barely three years following its IPO in 2004, the company's stock price skyrocketed more than 700% to $520, and it is now estimated to be worth more than $160 billion.[26]

So what has made Google so successful?

Google first exceeded expectations with its search engine innovations. PageRank and Hypertext-Matching Analysis technologies enhanced its algorithm to offer a search performance superior to any other search engine on the market.[27] Unlike existing search engines, which often failed to produce good matches to keywords, Google's search algorithm was able to pull out the most relevant pages and display them at the top of the results page.[28] It was also able to filter out sponsored sites that were deemed irrelevant and even irritating by internet users.

Besides the ability to return relevant results, the time taken to return those results is also an important functional attribute of a search engine. Instead of stocking up on large industrial servers that slowed under peak usage, Google deployed a network of linked PCs that allowed it to comb billions of sites and return results in a fraction of a second. With search capabilities that exceeded existing expectations, Google was able to turn this functional contact point into a Wow point.

Having attained leadership in online search, Google then capitalized on its technological innovations and large user base to build the company's most lucrative business to date—online advertising.[29] Google effectively transformed the online advertising industry when it introduced keyword-targeted advertising in 2000, known today as AdWords. Unlike traditional online advertisements, keyword-targeted advertising matches search keywords to relevant ads. These are then displayed alongside the search results.[30] As result, consumers received ads and deals that interested them, and advertisers were able to gain access to a targeted audience. Beyond this, advertisers were also delighted not to have to pay Google any fees until someone clicked on their ads.

In a 2005 study conducted by the U.S.-based Search Engine Marketing Professional Organization, Google's AdWords emerged as the most widely used search advertising program, with 95% of the 553 companies surveyed having used it.[31]

Google continues to exceed the expectations of advertisers by introducing other innovations. In 2003, it launched AdSense, through which Google Network members could carry ads that were relevant to the content on their pages. Google shared the revenue generated from the ads with the member websites. Again, advertisers gained much greater access to their target customers, and members were happy to be able to monetize their websites.[32] By 2006, revenue from AdSense had topped $4.2 billion, or 40% of the company's total advertising revenue.

Determined to take keyword-targeted advertising to the next level, Google launched its flagship web-based mail service, Gmail, in 2004. Using AdSense technology, relevant ads were now displayed adjacent to mail messages. The addition of Gmail to existing advertising avenues opened up more opportunities for advertisers to reach their target audiences. In order to attract a large email user base, Google came up with offers aimed at exceeding their expectations. For instance, it offered 1 gigabyte of storage space, 500 times more than the 2 megabytes then offered by Microsoft's Hotmail service. Gmail also contained other useful and practical functions, such as the grouping of email exchanges into conversations, and a powerful built-in search function to retrieve any email from the user's inbox. Gmail also offered the speediest email service available then, with instant appearance of the message on the receiver's screen.[33] These and other compelling built-in functions helped Google's Gmail exceed its users' expectations and outshine its rivals.

Google continues to attract more users and build up its advertising business by coming up with novel and innovative products.

!

"A great brand taps into emotions. Emotions drive most, if not all, of our decisions. A brand reaches out with a powerful connecting experience. It's an emotional connecting point that transcends the product."[1]

– Scott Bedbury, former Chief Marketing Officer of Starbucks

chapter 6

Emotional Contact Points Invoke Some Degree of Emotional Attachment to the Brand

This emotional attachment could be customer loyalty or, more desirably, a love for the brand. Unlike functional contact points, there is no reliable way to measure how an emotional contact point contributes to the overall value of the product or brand. Brands must consciously want to improve the user experience in order to identify what would improve it. If a brand is not in this state of mind, the brand cannot look at itself from the consumer's viewpoint. However, brands seeking to improve their emotional contact points have to be aware that the initiatives they take may not be universally appreciated. This is due to the essence of emotional contact points. The iPod, despite its award-winning design and note worthy performance, has its critics. Its popularity has caused people to turn against it, spawning websites, such as smashmyipod.com. Starbucks has also been on the receiving end of some amount of criticism. Its critics state that it is exorbitantly priced and that its menu is pretentious. Yet both these brands remain strong because they understand that they should concentrate on cultivating the loyalty of the people who really matter and not expend undue energy trying to convert all detractors.

Our Wowability Factors Survey found a correlation of 0.85 between Emotional Value and Exceeding Expectations. For companies like Nokia and McDonald's, the correlation between the two was even higher. Although correlation does not prove causality, anecdotal evidence supports the intuition that these companies have exceeded expectations through the strength of their emotional value. More details on the study and methodology employed can be found in Appendix 1.

Figure 6.1: Exceeding Expectations vs. Emotional Value

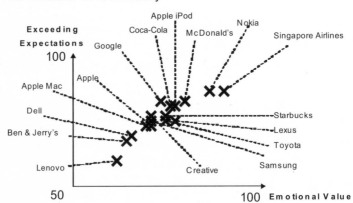

	Apple iPod	Apple Mac	Ben & Jerry's	Coca-Cola	Creative	Dell	Google	Average
Apple								
0.78	0.78	0.94	0.92	0.92	0.91	0.82	0.92	
Lenovo	Lexus	McDonald's	Nokia	Samsung	Singapore Airlines	Starbucks	Toyota	
0.92	0.48	0.94	0.92	0.92	0.75	0.82	0.79	0.85

Companies need to devise ways to increase the value of their emotional contact points, but before the methods can be appreciated, we must look at the essence of some major emotional contact points and their roles.

Price

Price may not seem to belong to the category of emotional contact points since it is both quantifiable and comparable. However, beyond the functional attribute of allowing consumers to buy the product, price actually holds more potential to create emotional value than immediately apparent.

A major role of price is as an indicator of quality. Goods that are more expensive are believed to be of higher quality than those that are priced lower. Regardless of the accuracy of this perception, the emotional value of the more expensive brand rises in the minds of consumers.

Products that create Wowability by having a premium price are positioned as luxury goods. Keeping in mind that the higher price invariably increases quality expectations, the brand must ensure that its products are indeed able to meet these higher expectations. Failure would disappoint consumers, who may then switch brands.

The pricing of luxury brands, such as Prada, Porsche, Hilton Hotels, and Oakley supports this theory. Even Bianchi Prada, daughter of the luxury brand's founder, agreed that its products were "unbelievably expensive."[2] Yet the "Wow" that Prada can incite in consumers indicates that there must be something about the quality of its products that allows it to sustain such pricing. Although Prada handbags carry a stiff price tag, its customers feel that the price represents quality. This is a classic example of a luxury brand using price as an indicator of quality and exceeding consumer expectations in that contact point to generate Wowability.

Another role price plays as an emotional contact point is in creating the idea of value for money. A product is seen as reasonably priced or "underpriced" if it costs less than what consumers believe it should. The brand then gains emotional value, and it is seen as benefiting the consumer and not just profiting from the sale. But there is no easy way of doing this as pricing decisions are affected by the costs faced by the company. However, by consistently reinforcing this strategy, the brand continues to add to its total value.

Sales and price promotions are another method to make consumers perceive that products are being offered for less than they are worth. The crowds attracted to sales are proof that these events do create such perceptions. Sales may also entice consumers to buy something they would not buy under normal conditions. Besides creating the idea that the products are underpriced, sales give the impression that the lower prices are available only for a limited period. This adds to the emotional value of the product. Consumers see the buy as a victory of sorts, having acquired greater value for their buck than they would have if they had bought it outside the sale period.

Brands can also exploit "reference pricing." In a supermarket setting, for example, customers tend to remember the price of only a few items. If a brand lowers the prices of these items, it creates an overall perception of high value, adding to the brand's total value and leading to Wowability if the brand has added enough value to exceed consumer expectations.

Dynamic pricing is another, albeit somewhat precarious, tactic. When Coca-Cola experimented with vending machines that increased the price of its drinks in tandem with the temperature,[3] consumers may still have felt that an ice-cold Coke was worth the higher price. However, there is likelihood that they felt taken advantage of and that the move to increase prices appeared unfair. This would have reduced the emotional value of the brand as consumers developed a perception that Coca-Cola was opportunistic and greedy. On the other hand, if, in line with dynamic pricing, prices were lowered when a product was most needed, it would actually add value to the brand.

Customer Service

"**Rule Number 1:** *The customer is always right.*
 Rule Number 2: *If the customer is ever wrong, re-read rule number 1.*"[4]
- Institute of Customer Service

It takes effort to Wow your customers, but you can certainly do it with customer service. For many brands, especially online brands like Amazon.com, this represents the only human contact the brand has with its customers.

When Toyota researched the luxury car segment, it found that its target customers were dissatisfied with the level of customer service they received.[5] When launching the Lexus, the Japanese automaker decided to leverage customer service in addition to superior performance and value to differentiate itself from entrenched players like Mercedes and BMW. Some 560 Lexus sales and service staff underwent training that involved extensive education about the new car, as well as multiple "soft skills" to allow them to offer better service to the customer.

Customer service spans a broad spectrum of activities. For the sake of clarity, let's divide this into pre-purchase, point-of-purchase, and post-purchase service.

Pre-purchase Service

This is a key stage of customer service and ranges from responding to product or service enquiries to assisting with product trials. Lackluster service can turn customers off while an excellent salesperson can convince customers to choose the brand. As with other emotional contact points, it is difficult to prescribe guidelines on making customer service more enthusiastic, but there are some ways to achieve this effect. Wal-Mart, for example, conducts a daily "Wal-Mart Cheer" to prep employees for the challenge of putting the customer first.

Nordstrom, a retail store renowned for its excellent customer service, has a rather straightforward method to ensure that its customers are afforded the best pre-purchase service. Bruce Nordstrom, chairman, believes that "we can hire nice people and teach them to sell, but we can't hire salespeople and teach them to be nice."[6] The company hires people who can connect with potential customers, understand their needs, and try their best to help them, never pushing a sale. "Hire the smile, train the skill" summarizes Nordstrom's hiring philosophy.

Point-of-Purchase Service

Once the customer is convinced to buy the product, it is the path of least resistance simply to direct him to the cashier. An issue of concern is the security of payment, especially with online shopping. Providing a secure method of payment is an important contact point at the point of purchase that adds to the emotional value of the brand.

Post-purchase Service

While the first two stages of customer service determine the completion of the sale, it is the post-purchase service that determines if the customer becomes a repeat buyer. A customer might experience Post-Purchase Cognitive Dissonance, which occurs when there is incompatibility between two cognitions.[7] The antagonizing cognitions may be "the notebook computer has the best features available in the market" versus "it looks bad!" Any form of discomfort from using the product after purchase has the potential to cause what is called buyer's remorse, and post-purchase customer service has a big role to play in minimizing any disappointment with the brand.

Customer service requires a willingness to answer any queries on the use of the product, facilitating a seamless transition from customer to satisfied user. The brand can also survey customers post-purchase to see if they are happy with their purchase. This conscious affirmation increases consumer affinity with the brand. These two systems could increase the emotional value of the brand by giving consumers the feeling that they are truly valued by the company.

Post-purchase service is prevalent in the financial services industry where financial advisers tend to maintain close contact with their clients. Since these professionals know from previous dealings what their clients are looking for, they can recommend services suited to those requirements. Clients are happy to give first preference to these financial advisors provided they were happy with their initial performance.

User Experience

The user experience is the emotional contact point that is probably hardest to quantify or describe. This is what users feel when they use the product or service. It is different from performance because the latter is quantitative—100mph in less than 5.8 seconds, for example—but the user experience is inherently qualitative.

User experience melds the various aspects of the product into a general feel the consumer gets from owning or using it. It is not the result of any one particular contact point. Instead, it is the general theme that results from the product as a whole. Although user experience is made up of a multitude of contact points, it still qualifies as a contact point in its own right: It is the intangible quality of creating a unified message through the balancing and juxtaposing of contact points.

User experience is relative. What may be fantastic to one customer may be distasteful to somebody else.

We can see the difference in the expectations of a Toyota customer versus those of someone who buys a Lamborghini. The Toyota customer expects a smooth ride, with easy steering and nifty features to make the daily drive to work a pleasant experience. The top speed rating is just a gauge of the car's power, and the owner is unlikely to actually want to hit it.

By contrast, the Lamborghini owner is probably after a more extraordinary user experience. The customer wants to hear the engine purr when it is idle, and roar when he hits the accelerator. It's all part of the experience, from the looks he receives as he steps out of the car in front of a posh restaurant, to the ease of overtaking other cars on the highway and seeing them disappear in the rear view mirror. These snapshots all contribute to the overall user experience.

Take Ben & Jerry's ice cream as another example. A glance at the company's website shows the positioning of the brand as colorful, fun, and youthful. The packaging of the ice cream coupled with the wacky names assigned to flavors build up expectations of a unique experience. Because Ben & Jerry's is also able to provide the experience it promises, the brand sells well despite the premium price.

In the premium segment of the ice-cream industry, filled with brands like Haägen-Dazs and Minghella that try to project a European image, Ben & Jerry's offers a different sort of experience. It offers consumers a feeling of fun and childlike indulgence rather than luxury. Consumers are generally amused by names like Chubby Hubby, Phish Food, and Chunky Monkey[8] and look forward to a great experience eating the ice cream.

Ben & Jerry's also has a track record of community service. Its flavor American Pie is tied to a promotion aimed at raising awareness about America's children. On its website, it states, "How can our nation be satisfied to lead the industrialized world in nuclear weapons technology, while falling behind other nations in caring for our children? Urge Congress to redirect spending priorities to invest more in America's children."[9] Ben & Jerry's community work is well publicized and has been effective in increasing consumer goodwill for the brand. It is seen as doing much more than what consumers could reasonably expect from an ice-cream brand.

As important as the development of the product is the need to define the kind of user experience brand owners want the brand to deliver. Consumers can usually tell if a product was developed without a clear focus on the user experience. Features don't blend well with the design, and the product does not have a unifying theme. We see examples of this among the smaller players in the mobile phone industry.

With big brands like Nokia, Samsung, and Motorola rapidly incorporating the latest technology, smaller brands struggle just to keep up. Concentrating on technology alone results in mobile phones that are just that: plain old mobile phones. These brands can't deliver any distinguishable user experience. They can't achieve Wowability.

Nokia and Samsung communicate the user experience in themed advertising; for example, showing the phone as an extension of a fun-loving personality, or as an accessory that makes the user appear more professional. Successful brands in many other industries also concentrate on the user experience. Coca-Cola's user experience can be seen in its slogan, 'Always Refreshing.' For Lexus, it is the relentless pursuit of perfection. The mediocre brands, however, seem clueless about what they want their customers to experience. Offering discounted prices, the preferred strategy among smaller brands, is only a short-term advantage since consumers have very little incentive to stay with these brands. As consumers become more sophisticated and are exposed to brands that promise a unique user experience, they are easily persuaded to switch. Even small brands can achieve Wowability in the long run by concentrating on the kind of experience they wish to offer their customers. Creating a Wow point at this contact point allows a brand to differentiate itself decisively from its competitors and build long-term competitive advantages.

Branding

The brand as a whole is a contact point, but there are also aspects of a brand that are contact points in their own right. The brand name, brand story, and brand leader are among such contact points.

Brand Name

Brand names, logos, and sub-brands all play a part in forming an image of the brand. A general rule is to avoid names that may have potentially negative connotations. Take Adidas for example. The brand name came from the founder's nickname Adi (short for Adolf) and the first three letters of his last name, Dassler.[10] Imagine what would have happened if the founder's first name, Adolf, had been used instead. It would probably not have become as successful if it had been linked—however irrationally—to Adolf Hitler, especially since the brand name was registered in 1948 when World War II was still an open wound. The brand has since grown into one famed for its sports apparel. A well-received brand name builds rapport with the consumer and can add to the emotional value of the brand. However, this is just the beginning. Most brand equity is built quite slowly as consumers begin to associate the brand name with certain qualities. Thus a good brand name is a necessary prerequisite to, but not a guarantee for, successful branding.

Brands like Ben & Jerry's, Gatorade, and Crayola have fancy names for their products. Are these names effective? A study published in the *Journal of Consumer Research* in 2005 analyzed the effect of color and flavor names on consumer choice.[11] It found that consumers encountering an interesting color description, antique red for example, would try to rationalize why the color had been so described. When consumers encountered a product before being aware of how its color was described, they derived greater satisfaction when discovering a description that matched the actual color: for example, cherry red or leather brown. Conversely, they were less satisfied by the product when the given name had little to do with the actual color. The implication is that if a product has a unique name for a particular color or flavor, satisfaction is greatest if there is synergy between the two.

Brand Story

Brand stories can be interesting contact points, but they are mostly neglected. They contribute to the brand by making it more relevant and memorable to consumers. Brand legends establish an emotional connection with the consumer. We are amazed by the tale of how Michael Dell set up his fledgling computer company in 1984 with nothing more than $1,000 and an idea.[12] That idea, which was to sell computers directly to customers, cutting out the middleman, enabled Dell to grow into the computer giant it is today. In 2006, Dell shipped more than 10 million systems in a single quarter, setting a new record for the company,[13] and showing how far it has come. Dell's brand story has played an important part in its success. Many brands have used brand stories to engage the consumer, with varying success.

Not all successful brands emphasize their brand story. Not many people know of Coca-Cola's origins or its story, but the brand is strong without it. Perhaps, the brand managers feel that the story of how Coca-Cola capitalized on trends in the cola industry would not interest the average consumer. Still, if your brand has a potentially interesting story behind it, you may want to consider leveraging this to allow consumers to better connect with your company. The internet has made it easier for brands to talk about their history and communicate to consumers just how they came about. From Adi Dassler to Colonel Sanders of Kentucky Fried Chicken, consumers are finding it easier to learn brand stories.

Kentucky Fried Chicken (KFC) has always tied the brand's image closely to Colonel Harland Sanders, the founder of the company. His image forms the logo of KFC and statues of a smiling Colonel Sanders extending his hand out to customers can be seen in KFC outlets around the world. On the KFC website, you can read about how he started the business, and how he was made a colonel in 1936 although he had never served in the army. On Ben & Jerry's website, you can read about how Ben Cohen and Jerry Greenfield met and started the business in May 1978, and how they grew it with an emphasis on balancing profit with social responsibility. Adidas' brand story was refreshed in a 2002 advertising campaign that featured old Adidas running shoes, soccer boots, and the like.[14]

The main aim of a brand story is to provide information about the brand, and show the aims and values the founders had in mind when setting up the business. A good brand story should be consistent with the brand's positioning. If your brand's positioning is as a producer of innovative technology, you should not confuse your consumers with stories that have nothing to do with innovation or technology. Many brands have brand stories just for the sake of having them. The generic story for such brands goes something like, "Mr. XYZ had a vision one day and started the brand. After numerous failures he decided to sink all of his resources into Brand ABC and the result is what you see today." Granted, not every founder can be as interesting as Walt Disney, Richard Branson, or Steve Jobs. Nevertheless, to turn this contact point into a Wow point, you will need to look for something different in your story.

By highlighting its unique aspects, the brand ensures that people will be reminded of it when they come across things related to the story. Also, having a vivid story about the people behind the brand gives it a human touch.

Brand Leaders

Closely linked to the brand story, the leaders of a brand also help make the brand more relevant to the consumer. They appeal to the consumer on a personal level, building emotional ties between the brand and its target audience. People remember Richard Branson as the adventurous billionaire and for his high profile business endeavors.[15] They also associate him with Virgin, a group that has grown to include more than 200 companies since it began life in the early 1970s. The Virgin brand has certainly benefited from Branson's personality.

Award-winning director and filmmaker Steven Spielberg is one of few moviemakers who can guarantee long lines of moviegoers excited about watching his movies. Highly successful movies like *E.T.*, *Gremlins*, and *Jurassic Park* have secured his place in the hearts of moviegoers, and his reputation now plays no small part in his box office successes. It is not often that people go to the movies for the man behind the screen, but Spielberg's penchant for making movies that tug at the heartstrings has precisely that pull effect on audiences.

Steve Jobs is synonymous with Apple, and the results he has achieved since returning to the company in 1996 have truly been astounding. Prior to its acquisition by Disney in January 2006, he was also at the helm of Pixar, the animation studio that produced blockbuster hits like *Toy Story* (1995), *Monsters Inc.* (2001), *Finding Nemo* (2003), and *The Incredibles* (2004). He is also a member of Disney's board of directors, in addition to being the company's largest single shareholder with a 7% stake.[16]

However, Jobs has always been more visible in the public eye with Apple than with Pixar or Disney. His influence in transforming Apple into a brand that stands for creativity in the fast-moving tech industry is phenomenal. He himself embodies the qualities of Apple, and from his speeches and media presentations, it is hard not to be Wowed by him. Apple's presentations often attract wide media coverage, partly because of the high interest in new Apple products, and partly to see master presenter Steve Jobs take the stage. He is confident and charismatic. He is just as interesting explaining the technical details of Apple's products as he is relating a story to the audience. Everything about his keynote address fits with Apple's brand image: a sleek presentation style coupled with entertaining and electrifying illustrations.[17] In many of his presentations, Jobs exceeds the expectations of his audience by unveiling an unexpected new product or an extension of an existing product line. This ends his speech on a high note, and people generally leave impressed with both Jobs and Apple.

Having a leader with charisma who acts as a spokesperson for the brand can bring it closer to consumers. A significant amount of emotional value is added through this contact point when consumers believe that if the brand leader is so passionate about the products, the brand must have a range of wonderful products. The brand now has a face and a personality.

Brands should bear in mind that succession can become an issue if the leader proves so influential that no one can fill the vacuum when he or she eventually steps down. One of the concerns about Apple is that it has not made known its plan for a successor to Jobs. This is worrisome, especially since Jobs underwent an operation to remove a tumor in his pancreas in 2004.[18] Apple has maintained that it does have plans in place for Jobs' eventual departure but has declined to divulge any details.[19] Whoever succeeds Jobs, Apple will have to think hard about how to present its new leader to the world. Will he or she be as charismatic and be able to handle major presentations with similar flair? Or will the new leader retreat into the background, letting someone else from Apple's top management do the talking?

Clear succession plans should be laid out for the long-term benefit of the brand and company. Take General Electric for example. Former CEO Jack Welch went through a lengthy and well-documented process to pick the company's new CEO. Eight years ago, he set up a three-way competition to determine his successor, with Jeffrey Immelt emerging the winner.[20] This is partly because passing of the baton has been an integral part of GE's culture, dating back to the late 19th century. For management, it is important to know that while having a charismatic leader can add value to the brand, it is also important to prevent over reliance on the current leader of the company.

Design

Design is one of the most important points of differentiation for a brand. Be it advertising, the product itself, or the brand logo, design can really Wow consumers. Design is visual, and a great design will draw attention to the brand even before consumers know anything about its functional contact points. Design is highly emotional. It entices the buyer to seek more information about the product. If powerful emotions are incited, they can increase the emotional value of the brand beyond expectations, allowing it to gain Wowability.

What constitutes great design? Unfortunately, there is no fixed answer. Design can, on one hand, stem from a highly functional objective. Xbox game console controllers took into account the shape of the human hand and designed the controller for maximum comfort during gaming. Design can also be largely emotional. Designing a cool logo that is etched in the consumer's memory is one example. But how does a brand know if it should focus on the functional or emotional objectives of design?

The answer really depends on the objectives of the brand, but what is certain is that great design melds both functional and emotional aspects, creating a holistic feel that consumers intuitively respond to. Very often, it is not the design of each individual part that is crucial, but rather how these parts interact to give an overall impression. Consumers do not look at the design of the button on a shirt but get an overall impression of the shirt. Gestalt, meaning that the whole is greater than the sum of the parts, is important in design.

Coming up with great design can require relatively little investment, or be extremely expensive. Either way, it is not easy to achieve. As with other emotional contact points, the key is careful thought.

A great design template is also a long-term investment as it can be used in future products. Although this is rare, such designs have the potential to become valuable assets for the brand. Used poorly, however, they can also backfire. One can compare Volkswagen's New Beetle against BMW's MINI to better understand this aspect of design.

Both designs were based on popular vehicles of yesteryear, but while one earned rave reviews, the other received scathing criticism. For consumers who were children when they first sat in the original Beetle or Mini Cooper, these new versions represented an opportunity to relive their childhoods without forsaking modern technology. The original Mini Cooper was manufactured by British Motor Corporation and was smaller than BMW's MINI[21] because part of the allure of the original was its petite size. Although BMW based its design on the original Mini Cooper, it overlooked an important aspect of that design. Thus the emotional value that could have been garnered was lost.

Volkswagen, on the other hand, has marketed the New Beetle well, and its strategy is epitomized in one of its ad slogans: "We have kept the shape. Until the very end."[22] A sense of nostalgia is what has driven many to buy the New Beetle, and Volkswagen has tried to retain that magic. A humorous series of ads in its campaign pokes fun at the original Beetle's shortcomings and promises to marry modern driving technology with tradition so that people can experience the joy of sitting in a car they dreamed of driving as children, and have a comfortable drive at the same time. The Beetle is so steeped in pop culture that a game children play, "punch buggy,"[23] would not have existed if not for the original Beetle.

A great design is something that consumers immediately recognize. Over time, brands that are renowned for their wonderful design can use more than just their products to convey this impression. Every single visual aspect of a brand can be used as an extension of design. In fact, it is more effective if the consumer sees a comprehensive design that is percolated through various contact points. Advertising, store layout, product design all need to have a unifying theme so as to allow the brand to come through strongly and differentiate itself from the crowd.

Design is a dynamic, ever-evolving art where conventions are regularly broken and new ones established. As with other emotional contact points, brands need to think through design carefully if they want to use it to add to their total value. Design can connect with consumers and tap into certain emotions.

Nokia's Wow Story

Design was the main force that helped Nokia move from playing catch up to Motorola and Ericsson, to its current position as the world's biggest mobile phone manufacturer.[24] Nokia's Wowability is difficult to deny. It has remained among the world's top 10 brands for nearly a decade.[25] Over that time, its value has increased significantly. More importantly, it has managed to remain on top of the competition. Nokia controls more than one third of the market today, claiming a 39% stake in 2007.[26]

The mobile phone industry is notoriously quick at adopting technology, and all brands have to be aggressive about keeping up to date. This means that Nokia's success cannot depend on technological prowess alone, as any Wowability that developed would be swiftly eroded by competing brands. The management team behind Nokia used design to build emotional value as they knew that they could not compete on functional attributes. This is not to say that the brand has not kept up with the latest that technology has to offer. Its N5200 and N5300 models boast VGA camera ability with 4x digital zoom, video camcorder functions, FM receivers, audio abilities, and many other functions to rival anything else on the market. The N93 is also able to record videos with DVD-like quality. Although Nokia knew that focusing on functional attributes would not give it first preference status, it kept up with the latest in technology to prevent other brands from depleting its brand bank balance and ensured that its functional value was also maintained. But it knew that design was where the future lay.

> ## "Nokia understood that the mobile would be a fashion accessory."
> - The Nokia Revolution, Dan Steinbock[27]

As consumers, it's an easy decision to buy a different brand simply because we do not like a tiny design feature. As a brand, it is a Herculean task to design a product that everyone will buy. Winning over a third of the market makes Nokia a brand well worth studying.

Never Be Satisfied—Push the Limits

A brand that hopes to achieve Wowability has to recognize that it cannot spare any effort in the quest for perfection. This mindset must be applied at all levels and in every aspect of the brand. For the Nokia design team, this sentiment is very much alive. Frank Nuovo, the chief of design for Nokia between 1995 and 2006, made it clear that his designers should "never fall in love with their first idea."[28] It can always be improved. His design team has been known to ruminate on details like the information to be displayed on the LCD screen. The dedication shown by the team won them the "Red Dot" Best Design Team Award in 2003. The annual Red Dot awards rank among the world's largest and most renowned design competitions.

The Thinking Behind the Design

Nothing about Nokia's designing process can be replicated with complete success. But by breaking down the process, we can distill its general strategies, namely believing that design is an integral part of the business, keeping the human quality, and looking at the phone as a fashion accessory.

By the time the 1990s had rolled in, the design standards in the mobile phone industry were in serious need of improvement. One of the reasons for Nokia's leadership is that it rose to the challenge. In 1990, Nokia established the three key concepts that set the direction of its nascent design strategy[29]— identifiable, global, and soft design language. Having a firm direction and focus has strengthened the brand's identity. When a person looks at a Nokia phone, he can easily identify it. It evokes any emotions from past experiences with Nokia. Nokia's global design team currently has 300 members of 34 different nationalities.[30] Included in this group are designers, psychologists, researchers, anthropologists, engineers, and technology specialists. The design team is responsible for exploring new materials, colors, and design trends in order to stay ahead of the competition. Nokia recently opened a design studio in India. The mix of cultures, traditions, and color in the country were attractive attributes that Nokia believed they could benefit from.

Nokia also wanted to ensure that the human factor was always kept in mind. Each mobile phone was designed with a specific target in mind. The Nokia 5xxx series was designed for the "sporty consumer." In addition to the standard capabilities, it also had a workout schedule and could keep track of training data and the number of calories burned. The phone body itself was capable of withstanding bumps, dust and water splashes.

The Nokia 6xxx series on the other hand was designed for the business user. The exterior was not as flamboyant as the 5xxx or the 7xxx series. It had a more serious look. The phone also supported Blackberry email so that the user could stay updated.

Consumers were impressed to find phones so well suited to their specific needs as opposed to the vast majority of phones available on the market. When Nokia was able to offer specific products across various niche segments, the brand gained overall Wowability.

Another thought that shaped Nokia's designs was to make the phone a fashion accessory. Nuovo consciously pushed Nokia's design to be more fashionable, drawing inspiration from fashion shows and the latest trends. The introduction of the 8xxx series legitimized its claim: Vogue magazine declared the 8860 to be the "first fashion phone" in its May 2001 issue. The phone sported a chrome finish and a cover that slid out to reveal the keypad. Simply holding the phone attracted attention to its owner. The clean lines and curves emphasized its elegance, and the phone was the perfect accessory to any outfit. Designing the phone with fashion in mind led to a line of trendy Nokia phones. Emotional value grew as consumers saw the phone not only as a communications tool but also as something that made them look stylish. This really exceeded their expectations of what a mobile phone was supposed to be.

Not only were Nokia phones good to look at, but with award-winning composer Ryuichi Sakamoto creating ringtones and other alert sounds for some models,[31] Nokia had a new way of attracting attention to the user. This took the brand yet another step beyond being just a phone to becoming a way for the user to appear sophisticated.

Drawing Inspiration

Nokia regularly draws ideas from other disciplines. This allows it to add unique features and details to its designs, turning them into Wow points. Nokia's designers speak to architects, furniture designers, paint specialists, and even designers of plastics. The Nokia 8801, for example, had its designers working closely with watchmakers and even incorporated some jewelry-making techniques.

Alastair Curtis, Nokia's chief of design since 2006,[32] is like his predecessor, an advocator of "people watching." He is known to take public transport whenever he can to draw inspiration from the people who actually use the phones. He believes that "by observing people, you see the way they interact, the way they do things, the strange rituals that they have,"[33] and this knowledge can then be used to design the best phone for them.

Drawing inspiration from varied sources gives Nokia designs a unique feel. Consumers recognize this and allocate a large amount of emotional value to the brand.

AXE's Wow Story

"We do all our research among 18 to 24 year-olds. We know these are the guys we are talking to, and the message has to be very single-minded."

- Esther Lem, Vice President of Brand Development, AXE[34]

The "single-minded" user experience that AXE quite unapologetically focuses on is that of sexuality. By focusing on a user experience that appeals to its target group, young men between 18 and 24, AXE is able to add a significant amount of emotional value to its brand. It aims to make consumers believe that using AXE increases their chances with women. Here AXE also exceeds consumer expectations with its simplicity. It consistently conveys through cool advertising, situations where a number of attractive women find a single man highly desirable simply because he uses AXE products. A particularly eye-catching advertising campaign launched by the brand in 2006 was the "Click" campaign.[35] The purpose of this award-winning series was to distribute free clickers (like those used to count people in an amusement park line) to males who wanted to count how many females they could attract in a single day. The campaign was a great success: 2.3 million clickers were ordered from Axe's European website, and a further 350,000 were ordered by text message in the UK alone. Today, clickers are purchased online for more than $40 apiece.

Another AXE advertisement that conveyed the idea of being desired featured thousands of women running through a forest to reach a man shown applying AXE body spray.[36] The tagline was simply, "Spray more. Get more." While no one would actually believe that using the body spray would work just like this, the ad does add to the emotional value of the brand. Consumers feel that using AXE body spray will make at least some women more receptive toward them. These advertisements, by building on the perceived user experience, increased the emotional value of the brand.

AXE's messages are backed by its core functional value— deodorants are meant to give the consumer confidence. It has effectively used advertising, branding, and other contact points to turn user experience into a Wow point. This has given AXE Wowability and moved it higher on the brand preference ladder.

!

"People don't
want to be
'marketed TO';
they want to be
communicated
with."[1]

- Flint McGlaughlin, *publisher of the Marketing Experiments Journal*

chapter 7

Most communicational contact points have a good mix of functional and emotional aspects. They communicate the functional value of the product and try to develop an emotional connection with the consumer. Achieving Wowability in communicational contact points ultimately hinges on creativity, in both the choice of the medium used and the content of the message. When used appropriately and consistently, they fortify the brand's image and make it more desirable.

Generally, communicational contact points work at three levels:[2]

Cognitive: The consumer becomes aware of, or much more familiar with, the brand and its message.

Affective: Emotional bonds and relationships are created between the brand and the consumer. The consumer may also form new attitudes or change existing attitudes toward the brand.

Behavioral: The communicational contact point causes a change in behavior, increasing store walk-ins or encouraging telephone calls or emails, ultimately enhancing sales and market share.

Although marketers and corporations would like to see communicational contact points work much harder at the behavioral level, they are actually much more effective at the cognitive and affective levels. They mostly create behavioral change only indirectly, and even then, may take time to work.

There is nothing good or bad about this. It is merely the way communications and human behavior work. To speed up the process, we can make communications more tactical; for example, offering discounts through coupons to drive sales. But this may have a negative effect on the brand in the long term. Pure branding and tactical communications have to be carefully balanced.

A key thing to be aware of is the "curse of knowledge." Once we know something, we cannot imagine not knowing it.[3] This makes it very hard for us to convey information to those who don't know it. Our way of doing so subconsciously assumes that others will understand exactly what we are saying even if we convey this knowledge through general statements like, "We need to become the most efficient manufacturer." We may know exactly how to do that, with our experience and education, but unfortunately others may not. This knowledge, in a way, has "cursed" us to be ineffective communicators.

To avoid this, we need to be more detailed and precise in our communications, and use stories that are easy to understand and remember. This helps counter our assumptions and the curse of our detailed knowledge.

Just as lethal and just as hard to avoid is the curse of relevance, or the assumption that the communications will be interesting to the consumer just because they are relevant and interesting to the communicator.[4]

With this in mind, let us look at a few key communicational contact points.

Advertising

Advertising is important for brands because it is one of the few communicational contact points they can control, compared, for example, to word-of-mouth. Management can design and fine-tune its advertisements to portray the brand in a particular way. This is the most important redeeming quality of advertising, which is otherwise one of the most expensive communicational contact points.

Companies use advertising to position their brand, portray the desired brand image, and sometimes even as a hard sell. In this sense, communicational contact points are geared to maximize the product's functional value. Without advertising, your target consumer may not know that your brand exists; he may even have misconceptions about it.

Turning an Advertisement Into a Wow Point

An advertisement that becomes a Wow point can work wonders for a brand. In 1998, Budweiser launched its "Wassup" advertisements,[5] which were so memorable, they sparked a trend of people greeting each other with the Budweiser Wasssssuuuuppp!!! These advertisements were based on a two-minute film created by Charles Stone III. In his film, a few friends lounging on couches in front of the television kept saying "True" in the intonation later picked up by "Wassuup." Budweiser's advertising agency saw the film and hired Stone to adapt it into a campaign for the beer company. Stone initially auditioned hundred of actors for the advertisements, but ended up hiring the original actors from "True," including himself.

The distinctive themes of these ads and the variations that followed are crude, funny, and characteristically male. They spawned a series of spoofs, all done by Budweiser, featuring every group from children to financial-types. (The spoof with children featured them drinking glasses of milk and saying "Wassup.") These ads created a sense of camaraderie among Budweiser consumers, and this feeling was transmitted to real-life situations.

Budweiser's subsequent ads were just as creative, an example being a series with three frogs saying "Bud-wei-ser." The animated frogs so successfully caught the imagination of the public that they sparked off a whole merchandising program.[6] The beverage company developed T-shirts, computer screen savers, and other memorabilia that promoted the brand in everyday life and not just in advertisements. Both these Budweiser advertisements shared a quirky humor that consumers could immediately recognize. This beer brand has successfully used advertising to develop a tradition and a connection with its consumers.

Design plays an important role in communicational contact points. A well-designed poster and a hopelessly jarring one both catch the attention of the consumer. Consumers will see them, but how will they perceive the brands?

One common misconception among advertisers is that consumers read print ads like regular articles, left to right and top to bottom. But readers typically scan the entire print ad, starting with the dominating visual.[7] Print ads should communicate with the reader at two levels, at a glance, and at a deeper level. Scanning the ad takes three to five seconds and should ideally convey the key branding message, while a deeper look, which takes 10 seconds more, should convey the key supporting points. The entire page also needs to be taken in context because other messages on the page may affect how viewers perceive the ad.

In 2005, Johnnie Walker advertised its Blue Label blended scotch whiskey in a series of unique print ads in *Fortune* magazine. The ads teased the reader with some indiscriminate alphanumeric characters like A22 and A23 on the first page.[8] On the flip side, it was revealed that A22 and A23 represented the best seats at The Royal Opera House in Covent Garden, London. At the bottom of the page was Johnnie Walker's logo with that of Blue Label and the slogan "Our Most Exclusive Blend." Variations of the ad featured theatres and exclusive restaurants around the world, but all had a simple theme and clear message: Drinking Johnnie Walker's Blue Label was akin to having the most exclusive seats in the house.

Celebrity Endorsements

David Beckham, England's former national football team captain and ex-Real Madrid *galactico*, earned $27 million from June 2005 to June 2006.[9] Most of this income, in fact, came from brand endorsements, including adidas and Gillette. Companies that seek celebrities to endorse their brands try to look for a match in the celebrity's and brand's images. For example, getting David Beckham to endorse Adidas soccer shoes and apparel makes good business sense. The effectiveness of celebrity endorsements depends on the fit between the celebrity spokesperson and the brand.[10]

Another way of making celebrity endorsements work is by identifying the celebrity most popular with a brand's target customers, and linking this celebrity to the brand. Tiger Woods has endorsed non-sporting brands, such as American Express and Accenture. The reason for this is that a large proportion of these brands' customers are business people who admire Woods for his talent and mental toughness on the golf course. We see Accenture's print ads emphasizing Woods' tenacity on the course. "Extraordinary insights often come from uncommon perspectives. Go on. Be a Tiger."[11] This tagline is complemented by a visual of Tiger Woods contemplating his next shot. Two concepts, "high performance" and "innovation" are immediately brought to mind, the values embodied by Woods that the brand hopes will be transferred to it. The Chinese computer firm Lenovo signed up FC Barcelona football superstar Ronaldinho as its "Worldwide Brand Ambassador"[12] in 2006 in a move to link the brand with sports. FC Barcelona is a popular soccer club and Ronaldinho was FIFA world player of the year[13] for two consecutive years in 2004 and 2005. Yet whether consumers will transfer goodwill for the club and the player to the Lenovo brand remains to be seen. The brand, however, is broadening its association with sports: In 2006, it was the computing equipment partner at the Winter Olympics in Torino. It has since extended this partnership to the 2008 Beijing Olympics.[14]

At times, a celebrity is famous enough and the concept interesting enough to create Wowability for the brand. Who will ever forget the "match" between Muhammad Ali and his daughter Laila Ali in the 2004 adidas ad? The slogan at the end of the ad, Impossible is Nothing, was quickly transferred to adidas. During the 2006 World Cup, adidas ran a two-part ad featuring the top soccer stars of the day in a match with two soccer legends, Franz Beckenbauer of Germany and France's Michel Platini. The brand was the first to use technology to bring together the old and the new in a single match. It was like watching a concert of the Beatles playing with U2! Consumers watching the ad may not have known much about adidas' soccer shoes but were almost certainly glued to their screens watching the incredible moves executed by the best soccer players across time. Stargazing had never been so much fun.

Communicational Contact Points and the Internet

The internet allows information to be easily accessed regardless of geographic location. The ease with which information can be gathered presents both an opportunity and a challenge to brands. Good news travels fast, and bad news, even faster. Review sites, blogs, or even websites that are dedicated to bashing your brand can be easily set up and promoted. Brands have learned that it is very easy for negative opinion to spread in cyberspace, regardless of whether the claims are true.

But this also holds true for good news. Word-of-mouth, or word-of-mouse, can be an effective contact point. By turning customer service into a Wow point, Amazon.com made sure that online customers who were impressed then went on to recommend the website to their family and friends. Due to the internet's ability to relay messages in real time, as well as its ability to reach consumers on a worldwide basis, Wowability here becomes even more important.

Online Reviews

With websites like ZDnet.com and Harmony-Central.com offering a large database of reviews across several product categories, consumers now find it easier than ever to make comparisons. Reviews tend to concentrate more on concrete aspects like the range of colors available, processing speed, and so on. Because consumers make these reviews, they may concentrate more on product performance and the functional aspects of the user experience. Most people do not divulge their personal feelings when posting a review because people expect reviews to be more objective than subjective. Comments like, "I think the product is good because it makes me feel young when I use it," are not really useful to other consumers.

Problems with design are quickly pointed out; they may be identified through consumer feedback and complaints, or through third-party testing of the product. This information, which may have been overlooked by the brand, has an impact on the consumer's purchase decision.

In the past, reviews were mostly carried in magazines. "Experts" gave their opinions on a host of new products, listing the pros and cons of each. Although these reviews provided useful information, consumers still tended to take the ratings with a pinch of salt. Consumers are aware that many publications are subsidized by the ads they carry, which makes readers skeptical about their ability to remain objective.

Against this, an independent source, like a website where fellow consumers comment on specific product flaws (and strengths), seems much more credible. Very often, people who notice a flaw in a product point it out, sparking off a discussion on the issue. This way, consumers can judge for themselves if it is indeed a problem and how significant a problem it is.

An inherent danger for brands is that a disgruntled customer could give a scathing review, causing potential buyers to form a negative impression. This could be due to a faulty part, bad service, or just because someone dislikes the brand. The other danger of these online sites is the possibility that some of the postings may have originated from the marketer or a competitor.

Blogging

Everyone from the average teenager to professionals like management guru Tom Peters have blogs. Blogs have become a fascinating trove of information. A quick search on Google on any brand would almost certainly turn up a blog entry on it. Sometimes this is not a product review per se, but a more trivial post like, "I went to Janice's place last night, and she's got the Nokia N90!" Other times it could be an informal review of the product. As bloggers tend to write about events in their lives, purchasing a new digital camera could warrant a blog entry on the blogger's experience of the selection and buying process, as well as his initial experience with the product.

Similar to product reviews, blogs represent another source of brand information for consumers. The Unofficial Apple Weblog for example has one of the most extensive databases on Apple's products on the internet. The blog has information on new product releases as well as posts highlighting problems with Apple's products. For example, there is a post describing a problem with the Mac notebook.[15] Apparently, it makes a "moo-like" sound. A technician at Apple has explained that this is normal and is caused by the intermittent sound of the fan turning on and off to conserve power and dispel heat. Although Apple meant well when it incorporated the fan, the sound has been perceived as a problem by a group of consumers, and it influences their opinion of the product. This opinion is now easily communicated to other users and prospective buyers.

Review sites in the format of blogs are becoming more popular, with the informal nature of blogs making these reviews more personal. After each blog post, readers are invited to post their comments. Blogs are generally less organized than review sites like ZDnet.com, but regular readers may prefer this format because new blog posts are posted at the top, making it easier to follow the progress of the argument. Apart from this, the information can be considered just as trustworthy if readers perceive the contributors to be as credible as those posting on official review sites.

Word-of-Mouth

Word-of-mouth is information about a brand that is passed from one consumer to another. However, this definition could be expanded to include any independent person with information on the brand conveying it to another person. This would include employees whose job may not involve promoting the brand or strangers posting their comments on the internet.

The key attribute is how independent the person conveying the information seems to be. Credibility falls if you know the person telling you good things about the brand is a member of the sales staff. The way the information is conveyed includes written and oral communication, online or offline. Word-of-mouth is extremely important because consumers can get detailed descriptions of the product, including any defects that brand owners are either unaware of or deliberately do not mention in their communications. The internet has made word-of-mouth far-reaching and much easier.

How to Make Word-of-Mouth Work

A 2006 study conducted by Assistant Professor Carl Walter of Northeastern University investigated the effectiveness of professional word-of-mouth agents who disclosed their affiliation to consumers.[16] It found that a significant 75% of consumers did not mind that the people providing them with brand information were doing so as part of a commercial campaign. This was true as long as the representatives were perceived to be honestly providing information to help consumers make better purchasing choices. Interestingly, those who knew that they had been approached by representatives of the brand were more likely to spread the information to others compared to those who did not know. This study implies that as long as brands conduct these campaigns with integrity and transparency, consumers are willing to take the information at face value. In cases where there had been some misunderstandings about the brand, talking to the brand representative helped clear these doubts. This sometimes turns negative perceptions into positive ones.

However, creating a lot of marketing hype raises consumer expectations of your product. If your brand does not live up to these expectations, you may end up with disappointed customers who may then switch to alternative brands. In addition, a word-of-mouth campaign involves brand representatives going out to talk to people and providing information to potential customers. If the product has shortcomings and the brand representatives try to gloss over them, or worse, hide them, then the brand and its representatives will lose their credibility. If they want to be perceived as credible, then they should be upfront and honest with consumers. Consumers will get both sides of the story and will perceive the brand in its entirety. At the same time, this allows the brand to get valuable feedback from consumers who bring up areas in which it needs to improve. It may not be nice to hear bad things about your brand when you are trying to tell consumers the good things about it, but if you ensure a two-way communications channel, both parties can benefit.

Product Placement in Movies

Product placement has gained popularity with advertisers in recent years. We have seen a variety of products being showcased in movies, from luxury goods, such as the BMWs and Aston Martins placed in James Bond films, to bottled water. The Fiji water label has appeared in movies, such as *Rat Race*, and television shows, such as *Sopranos*, *Friends* and *Just Shoot Me*.[17] Product placement fees defray the costs of making a movie, although there has been criticism by those who feel that they distract viewers from the story, and that sometimes, parts of the movie have had to be altered to accommodate the brand or to provide enough "air time" for it.

A study published in the *Journal of Promotion Management* found that consumers tend to better recall brands that appear in a movie when the brand appears with the principal actor and is positively evaluated.[18] The study also found that "liking" is linked to how well consumers think the brand has been integrated into the scene. But the better integrated it is, the less likely it is to be recalled. In short, when consumers are distracted by the brand's presence in a scene, they will remember it, but the memory is attached to negative feelings. Conversely, if a brand fits nicely into the scene and does not jar, consumers will not mind its presence, but are likely to forget it since its exposure was so smooth they barely noticed it. This is also a very expensive option.

In a Blink—One-Second Advertisement

One-second advertisements, or blinks, have been developed by Clear Channel as a variation to the traditional 15-, 30-, 45- and 60-second radio advertisements. Examples of how these ads can be effectively used include the sound of a car horn followed by a male voice saying "Mini."[19] Brands with a recognizable sonic logo, like Intel, can use this medium between songs or other radio programs. The main aim is not to provide consumers with new information, but to serve as a reminder of the brand. There is, however, just enough time for the brand's name or signature tune to be heard, and there are concerns that consumers may not be able to immediately link the ad to the brand.

There are also concerns about the limitations of broadcast monitoring because monitors are only able to track ads that last more than five seconds. Their inability to track shorter ads makes it difficult for brands to confirm that their slots were aired, or to determine the exact time when they were aired.

As blinks are priced an estimated two to three times over what one sixtieth of a 60-second ad spot would cost,[20] it makes more sense for media owners to sell these slots over larger chunks. However, doing this would defeat their purpose because consumers facing 60 one-second ads would instantly switch off and not remember most of them. Blinks are designed to be placed individually between songs, programs, or other larger chunks of ads; they would lose their impact if played in succession with other blinks. A five-minute break consisting of

300 Blinks would be highly ineffective for all brands because consumers would not recognize or distinguish between the different brands in the random cacophony of sound.

In recent years, more research has been done to investigate how quickly consumers form opinions. The results have been astonishing. In 2006, a group of internet researchers analyzed the correlation between the time spent at, and the first impressions received of websites. They found that when asked to rate various websites, respondents exposed to a site for 500 milliseconds (half a second) assigned ratings that correlated to those of respondents allowed only 50 milliseconds, merely the blink of an eye.[21] First impressions are formed extremely quickly; we have only just started to understand how fast the human mind interprets information. This is not to be mistaken for subliminal messages where people do not actually perceive the message in the conscious mind. Blinks have the potential to cause consumers to sit up and say "What's that?" simply because these ads are different from other ads. But the ad has to be "loud" and recognizable enough for consumers to catch it; otherwise it fades into the background noise.

Advertisements on Public Transport

From buses to trains to taxis, public transportation and transport infrastructure have proven to be popular with advertisers. After all, anywhere large groups of people congregate are potentially good places to advertise in. But just how effective are these ads? A 2005 study published in the International Journal of Advertising[22] investigated the effects of advertising in and on taxis. It found that taxi ads attract interest from consumers across demographic groups, with ads carried on taxi tops and billboards on taxi doors scoring particularly well. Interestingly, although people may dislike certain forms of advertising, such as product placement, respondents were generally either neutral or positive about advertising in or on taxis. Perhaps advertisements help turn the ubiquitous taxis into curiously decorated cars that offer consumers some visual entertainment, particularly in a traffic jam. The study noted, however, that consumers tend not to notice new campaigns launched on taxis. This suggests that taxi advertising should be used as a secondary medium, to augment what people see on TV or other media.

Meanwhile, we have all seen posters of different shapes and sizes within trains and buses. Because these modes of public transport serve large numbers of people each day, advertisers see them as a great opportunity to disburse their messages. As more ads are put up, ad clutter increases within train stations, bus terminals, and in the vehicles themselves. The larger brands routinely have the entire train or bus plastered with just their ads, thus ensuring that whoever steps into the bus or train will only be exposed to their brand. Sometimes the fact that the entire train or bus (or even airplane) is covered by one gigantic ad is enough to exceed expectations and Wow people. The Goodyear Blimp is an icon to most people in North America, and the air ship successfully turns heads wherever it goes. The Goodyear brand has definitely benefited from these blimps, which grab attention when they fly by major sporting events or large concentrations of people.

Integrating the various communicational contact points and understanding them with the goal of turning them into Wow Points gives a brand an edge over its competitors. Too often, companies view promotions, PR, advertising, and other communications tools as separate, not realizing that they can be coordinated to present a strong, unified brand message.

Carl's Junior is one fast food chain that has demonstrated the ability to integrate various contact points to create Wowability. Although controversial, its 2005 advertisement featuring hotel heiress Paris Hilton promoting the spicy burger encompassed many Wow points. Hilton was chosen by the burger company to entice young males, its primary target market.[23] Because burgers are typically not endorsed by celebrities, especially scantily clad ones, this exceeded consumer expectations and generated publicity in the media. There were a number of news reports and multiple blogs about the advertisement, which the Parents Television Council of America wanted to remove from public television because of its sexually suggestive content. Carl's Junior responded by launching a website that showed the advertisement along with blog posts about it. This website ranked second in terms of web-hits in its category, and traffic to it was so heavy that it crashed in its first week.[24] This is an example of how one brand took its commoditized product's message of 'hot' to unexpected levels and seamlessly integrated its contact points to generate Wowability. Even today, "the Paris Hilton advertisement" continues to be a topic of conversation.

Coca-Cola's Wow Story

Coca-Cola claims the number one spot in the vast majority of markets it competes in, and has topped Interbrand's best brand rankings since 1998. A brand cannot remain at the top without having Wowability. In fact, consumers are so Wow-ed by the "The Real Thing" that the brand was valued at US$67 billion in 2006, an impressive US$10 billion over second-ranked Microsoft. [25]

Reducing Coca-Cola to its core product highlights the power of the brand. In essence, a "Coke" is simply a beverage that quenches the thirst while giving the consumer some satisfaction from its taste. That functional value could easily be derived from other, if not most, beverages in the market. It is also difficult to imagine that people would attribute so much emotional value to a product that they viewed as just a beverage. The success of Coke then must lie in something other than contact points that are largely functional or emotional. While a car would have functional and emotional value from contact points, such as fuel efficiency and design, the Coke brand has had to rely on communicational contact points to create value beyond that of a carbonated drink.

Coca-Cola's founders and management have been consciously aware since John Pemberton first mixed the beverage in 1886[26] that they needed to build and maintain the brand. This, ultimately, is the definitive factor that makes Coca-Cola the world's number one brand. Coca-Cola aptly utilizes its brand name, brand logo, print advertising, and other communicational contact points to associate its product with strong consumer emotions.

Brand Logo and Brand Name

A brand's logo and name may seem to be highly generic communicational contact points since virtually every product has a brand name and a brand logo. In addition, once the logo and name are finalized, they are harder to change than communicational contact points like advertisements. However, a consumer has to be aware of the brand name and logo before a brand bank can be created. All increments in value have to be allocated to a brand bank and that requires a brand name and logo.

The history of colas, and Coca-Cola in particular, began in the late 19th century, shortly after coca leaves were discovered to have a stimulant effect. Concoctions combining coca leaf extract with soda water were then sold as tonics. Pemberton mixed the coca leaf extract with kola nuts, which contained caffeine, and sugar, to create a headache remedy, or "Brain-Tonic," as it was initially marketed.[27]

A competent calligrapher, Pemberton wrote out the brand name Coca-Cola in cursive, which, rather unimaginatively, was derived from the main ingredients of the drink. The only change that he made was to replace the "k" in "kola" with a "c," giving the brand name a sense of balance. Bearing in mind that the drink was initially positioned as a "Brain-Tonic," that may have been a wise move, if not the most creative one. The cursive writing may have added a sense of respectability to the brand and this helped to reinforce its medicinal image.

The brand name proved so successful that it inspired an army of competitors with similar sounding names, some of which included "Cola-Ola," "Cola-Coke," and "Coca & Cola."[28] With so many such names in the market, the Coca-Cola brand could have been watered down and might have lost its identity in a short period of time. But Coca-Cola knew the importance of defending its identity and filed lawsuits against many of its imitators. One high-profile lawsuit that took years to resolve was filed against Chero Cola. In its lawsuit, Coca-Cola demanded that Chero Cola drop the word "cola" from its brand name.[29] It took nine years of legal wrangling before Chero Cola was actually ordered to remove the word "cola" from its advertisements. With the loss of its by then established brand name, the production of Chero was discontinued.[30] Coca-Cola's main aim was to defend its identity by defending the brand name. In 1910, the company filed a lawsuit against another imitator, "Koke." Again the legal battle spanned several years, but Coca-Cola won its case in the end, and Koke was ordered to drop the name and any related images.[31]

Having secured and defended the rights to its brand name, Coca-Cola then proceeded to ensure that it was highly visible and widely recognized, and that it became the choice "cola" drink. In other words, the brand name had to be marketed and advertised.

Advertising

Looking at Coca-Cola's advertisements, we can appreciate how well the brand has used this communicational contact point. While any brand with the right budget can use advertising to capture consumer attention, Coca-Cola has gone further. It tailors its communications to suit the aspirations of its consumers, ensuring that its messages reflect their needs and desires. This strategy has resulted in the continuing relevance of the brand.

When we think about the main message in Coca-Cola advertisements today, we can see that they center on satisfaction, fun, and camaraderie. These sentiments are rather different from the slogans of the early 1900s when Coke positioned itself as a medicinal tonic. Between 1900 and 1908 words heavily used in Coke's advertisements included "revives," "sustains," and "invigorates."[32] The slogan also declared that Coke was able to cure "headache and exhaustion." Clearly Coke used communicational contact points to highlight its benefits, the ideal strategy at a time when there was great conviction about the benefits of coca leaves and kola nuts. Coke used advertising to convey the idea that it really had the benefits that consumers sought, thereby increasing the perceived functional value of the brand.

With the influx of various similar-sounding names, Coca-Cola used advertising as a means of defending its market share. It was quick to incorporate taglines, such as "Demand the Genuine—Refuse Substitutes," and "Nicknames Encourage Substitutions" to prevent a dilution of its brand identity. By using the word "genuine" to describe itself and "substitutes" to describe other brands, it fostered an attitude that Coca-Cola was in fact the "real thing." The advertising resulted in consumers allocating emotional value to Coke for being the authentic drink. It also resulted in an increase in its functional value as the "genuine" Coke was perceived to have a better taste.

In 1914, World War I broke out. Around the same time, cocaine addiction came under scrutiny. Coke faced negative publicity since it contained trace amounts of the drug. Although the amount of cocaine in Coke was hardly enough to cause an addiction, Coke's advertising had to counter these negative associations. After the war, it also had to take post-war consumer sentiment into account.

Coke was by then firmly repositioned as a drink rather than a "tonic." Words, such as "refreshing," "sustains," and "invigorates" were dropped in favor of the word "thirst." Advertisements often depicted scenes of the beach to better depict Coke as the ultimate thirst quencher. The post-war period was characterized by an atmosphere of celebration, and these advertisements tapped into those sentiments to persuade consumers to choose Coke over any other drink. One of the advertisements also touted Coke as being as "wholesome" as water and even more satisfying. The fact that Coke was generally affordable and, at the same time, perceived to give consumers more satisfaction, made it a popular choice.

After the Second World War, however, consumer sentiment again changed. By that time, Coke had become adept at creating sensitive messages. Slogans now primarily promoted the use of a bottle of Coca-Cola as a means of making friends. Some of the slogans include, "High Sign of Friendship," "Happy Moment of Hospitality" and "A Moment on the Sunny Side."

Advertisements on television, newspapers, and magazines are common communicational contact points for most brands. Coca-Cola's success derives not so much from its use of these media as from tailoring its messages to suit the sentiment of the time. The moves that Coke took, and the advertisements that ran as a result, quickly increased its emotional value far above that of its rivals.

Alternative Communications

While most of its competitors and even marketers in other categories were using only print and television, Coke employed alternative forms of communication. In fact, Coca-Cola was one of the first few to think outside the box to grow its brand. The advantage of using such methods is that they are usually unexpected, and consumers' defenses do not stop them.

One alternative communicational contact point that Coke used heavily was merchandising. Some of the items that carried the Coke brand name included clocks, coasters, calendars, and trays. Today, Coca-Cola merchandise is an industry in itself, and popular online auction platforms, such as eBay list a large number of "antique" Coca-Cola branded items for sale. Since they were practical, shopowners had little reason not to display them. A consumer walking into a shop that was practically covered with the Coca-Cola logo and brand name must have found it hard to order anything else.

Another alternative communicational contact point that Coke used was painting its ads directly on prominent buildings in central locations. Its very first outdoor advertisement is still visible in downtown Cartersville, U.S., on the side of a pharmacy store. Painted in 1894, this large red and white advertisement is listed on the National Register of Historic places as one of the country's first outdoor building advertisements.[33] It attracts many tourists from around the world, and serves as a promotional tool for Coca-Cola.

Ben & Jerry's Wow Story

Ben & Jerry's has achieved Wowability with its high quality, decadently rich ice cream. Consumer expectations are exceeded when generous chunks of dough, chocolate, and fruit are discovered in the process of enjoying the ice cream. But the consumer experience of the brand begins much earlier, with the packaging that Ben & Jerry's has effectively converted into a communicational Wow point.

Ben & Jerry's ice-cream tubs are extremely colorful to begin with. The company is not afraid to use really bright colors, such as yellow and pink, even the occasional hint of purple, to give an almost cartoon-like look to the brand. Where luxury segment players have mostly opted for a European "feel," Ben & Jerry's has chosen to go with childlike images. A look at the tubs immediately communicates the offer of a fun experience, exceeding the expectations of consumers who have otherwise been exposed to more subdued, maybe even predictable, promises of indulgence.

In addition to being colorful, the packaging of each ice-cream flavor looks distinctly different from the rest. Again, this is a big difference from competitor brands, which have largely stuck to a design template. A feeling of "being a child in a candy store" is evoked as consumers encounter an amazing array of colors and flavors to choose from.

The packaging also carries the rather unusual names of the various ice-cream flavors. Some examples include Chunky Monkey, Karamel Sutra, and Phish Food. Consumers had never before come across such interesting names as competitor brands have tended to stick to rather drab descriptions of their ice-cream flavors. Thus, once again, the feeling of fun is communicated to consumers who are eager to discover what exactly is in that tub.

Ben & Jerry's packaging is a communicational contact point because it attracts attention to the brand in a similar way that other communicational contact points, like television advertisements and billboards, aim to do. Besides trying to add emotional and functional value to the brand while communicating a positioning or message, communicational contact points must also be able to grab attention in a market experiencing high degrees of brand proliferation. Ben & Jerry's packaging does exactly that. When looking at a freezer section filled with mostly dark brown or white ice-cream tubs, bright yellow Chunky Monkey and pink Cherry Garcia stand out, and consumers feel compelled to at least pick up the tub to find out more. This is a Wow point.

Packaging is not usually thought of as a communicational contact point, or at least not as a very important one. However, because Ben & Jerry's gave it due importance and forethought, they were able to use it to strongly convey their positioning and gain Wowability for the brand.

!

"The public is the only critic whose opinion is worth anything at all."[1]

– Mark Twain, American author

chapter 8

In this chapter and the next, we will explore some actionable yet quite simple tools and methodologies that can help brands achieve Wowability. These tools identify the specific contact points that brands should focus on and help brands formulate strategic plans that lead to Wowability.

The first is the Wow Score, a survey designed to discover the perception of, and overall sentiment toward, the brand. The results of this survey also provide a more concrete idea on which aspects of the brand have not been allocated enough resources. The second tool is the Wowability Test, which can be used by brands that do not have the resources to conduct a full survey. Its strength lies in its succinctness, and it can be completed by the brand's stakeholders in a relatively short period of time. The last tool is a methodology called the FAR Paradigm, which is based on the brand bank approach. It looks primarily at consumers' familiarity with the brand and suggests strategies that would allow the brand to develop a more loyal consumer base.

Tool 1: The Wow Score

The Wow Score is a survey that tabulates contact points based on how consumers prioritize them and the relative importance assigned to them. This is then compared against their perception of the brand's performance on each. The results are used to develop strategies for the brand to move toward Wowability.

Efficacy of the Survey

Brands should bear in mind that there are a number of factors that may reduce the Wow Score's efficacy or distort its results: namely, when an inappropriate group of brands is examined, an inappropriate group of contact points tested, or when an inappropriate group of people is selected to participate in the survey.

Getting the Appropriate Competitors for Inclusion

The brand's closest competitors should be included in the survey for comparative purposes. Determining if the competitor is a close one largely depends on how the brand defines its industry and if it competes in a niche market. For example, there would be a difference in who qualifies as a close competitor in the general apparel industry as opposed to the sportswear industry. These differences will have to be considered when selecting the competing brands to include.

Theoretically, the more competitors included in the survey, the more insightful the results will be. However, in practice, this may not work well because it makes the survey tiresome for the respondent, and he may end up filling in answers at random, affecting the true picture of your brand in the process. As a general rule, do not include more than five competitors in the survey.

Getting the Right Contact Points in the Survey

The dilemma for most managers is that a brand simply has too many contact points to be included in the survey. The hardest part of setting up the survey would be narrowing the list down to around 15. Ideally, there should be five contact points for each of the three categories—functional, emotional, and communicational. There may, however, be instances where brands may want to include more contact points overall or in a particular category.

Getting the Right People to Participate

The right people are simply the brand's existing or prospective customers. Their opinions are the only ones that matter. Getting the right people to complete the survey will ensure that the results are relevant.

The Structure of the Survey

The goal of this survey is to test for a number of things in order to arrive at an appropriate plan of action for Wowability. This includes the importance consumers assign to the various contact points of a brand, their familiarity with these contact points, and the level of expectations that have been exceeded by all brands. The contact points to be included can be determined by focus groups or through internal discussions among the brand's managers. Some consumers can be included in the latter. The set of contact points should remain the same in all sections of the survey.

My colleagues at ADK and I conducted a survey involving about 180 respondents where we compared three brands in the MP3 player industry: Apple iPod, Sony MP3, and Creative ZEN. For more details on this study, please refer to Appendix 1. We then tabulated the resulting Wow scores. Brands will have to customize the survey to suit their needs, but the main structure, comprising three distinct parts, should be maintained.

The first part of the survey establishes the importance consumers place on the different contact points of the products in a particular industry. The responses are then averaged. In our survey, the most important contact point selected by the consumers was "product features," which scored an average 6.3 out of a highest possible score of seven. This then becomes the "ideal" score, or in other words, the expected value that consumers look for. When assessed in isolation, this may have little use or may even be misleading, but when compared with statistics from the other parts of the survey, it has bearing on the buying decision.

The second part deals with familiarity. It asks consumers to note their level of familiarity with each brand's contact points. The individual scores are added and again averaged to yield an optimal score. Low scores in this section show that consumers have not had much experience with those particular contact points, and may indicate a potentially serious communications problem. The contact point may have tremendous value, but if consumers do not know about it, then the perceived value of the brand would still be low. In our survey, we found that familiarity with Sony's MP3 player was low, with nearly all of its contact points scoring around three out of a possible seven, compared to the iPod and Creative ZEN, both of which consistently scored above four. One reason for this could be that Sony's MP3 player is relatively new to the market compared to Creative ZEN and the iPod, both of which have been around for far longer and have launched extensive marketing campaigns.

The third section of the survey cuts to the crux of the matter and determines whether a contact point has exceeded the expectations of consumers. For the contact point of "Trade shows," the iPod outperformed its competitors as well as the ideal score with its score of 4.22, indicating that it exceeded expectations on this contact point.

Once the survey is completed, the results need to be tabulated and interpreted. As the survey also tests consumers' perception of other brands, we need to cross-tabulate the results for all brands to derive deeper insights.

The Results

The survey is designed to identify which contact points the brand should focus on to achieve Wowability most effectively. For a brand to know where it should concentrate its resources, it first needs to know which contact points consumers find important. It also has to know how familiar consumers are with each of its contact points, since better communications may prove to be the simplest solution to increasing its value. Finally, knowing if and by how much consumer expectations are being exceeded in a particular contact point allows the brand to decide if it is viable to invest resources in that contact point. For example, if the brand knows that it cannot match its closest competitor in one contact point, it may consider trying to exceed expectations in a different one.

Wow Score

Ideal scores are derived from the first section of the survey, which establishes the level of importance consumers assign to the various contact points. By tabulating the Exceeding Expectations score with Ideal scores, we can express the contact points that exceed consumer expectations as a ratio of the contact points that consumers consider important. In the table below, we have also classified the different contact points as functional, emotional or communicational. Wow Scores are derived by using the following formula:

(Average Score/Ideal Score) *100

Table 8.1: Wow Score Table

Contact Points	Average Score			Ideal Score	Wow Score		
	Sony MP3	Apple iPod	Creative ZEN		Sony MP3	Apple iPod	Creative ZEN
Features	4.56	4.88	4.61	6.30	72	77	73
Performance	4.51	4.82	4.61	6.25	72	77	74
Price	4.29	4.46	4.58	6.15	70	72	75
Design	4.54	4.96	4.51	5.60	81	89	81
Usage Experience	4.25	4.61	4.39	5.57	76	83	79
Customer Service	4.21	4.51	4.27	5.52	76	82	77
Leadership	4.11	4.37	4.09	4.41	93	99	93
Brand Story	4.03	4.31	4.06	4.36	92	99	93
Sales Promotions	4.29	4.66	4.43	5.72	75	81	77

Recommendations	4.23	4.49	4.42	5.61	75	80	79
Advertising	4.23	4.38	4.36	4.38	97	100	100
Trade Shows	4.16	4.22	4.17	4.14	100	102	101

So for example, to tabulate the Wow score of iPod's "Trade Shows" contact point, we would just divide 4.22 (iPod's average score on this contact point) by 4.14 (Ideal score of this contact point) and get 1.0193. We would then multiply 1.0193 by 100 getting a score of 101.93 which would be extended to the closest full number and thus stated as a Wow Score of 102 in this case.

Our study shows that for MP3 players, consumers place most importance on functional contact points like features, performance, and price. All three brands did fairly well in these contact points, with the iPod scoring the highest. The goal is to have as many contact points as possible with Wow Scores above 100, especially in the case of the more important ones. These are the hardest to attain high scores in, and they take considerable time and effort to boost. However, once a brand has established itself as the one with the highest Wow Score (above 100) for an important contact point, it has successfully created a Wow point, and it will be extremely tough for competitors to overtake it.

The results for all sections are averaged out, and the scores are used to provide an evaluation of the individual contact points. On their own, the different sections of the survey have limited use. But when taken together, the results become much more meaningful and actionable. Brands need to look through the scores of each contact point and, using the guidelines below, get a better understanding of how well they are performing on each. This will also give them an overall impression of where their brands stand with regard to competitors. Tracking scores will periodically allow the brand to see where they and their competitors are headed.

Contact Points Score Analysis Guide

(1) High Importance for Consumers, High Score in Familiarity, and High Score in Exceeding Expectations

This contact point is a valuable asset for the brand as consumers feel very strongly about its importance and believe that the brand offers the best value in it. But even if the brand is already doing well in a particular contact point, it has to continue to improve in order to maintain its Wowability.

If the brand notices this edge in a competitor's contact point, it would take a lot for the brand to exceed expectations here, and it would probably be more worthwhile for it to focus on other contact points.

(2) High Importance for Consumers, High Score in Familiarity, and Low to Moderate Score in Exceeding Expectations

Consumers are well informed about the contact point, and it is important to them, but the brand just does not have Wowability here.

Check how competing brands have scored in order to decide on a plan of action. If competitors have scored even lower, then there is a clear opportunity to focus on this aspect and turn it into a Wow point for the brand.

(3) High Importance for Consumers, Low Score in Familiarity, and Low to Moderate Score in Exceeding Expectations

The brand should try to increase consumers' familiarity with the contact point. The low to moderate exceeding expectations rating may stem from low familiarity rather than poor performance. The brand should first try to improve familiarity by using marketing communications tools like PR and advertising before initiating other plans to achieve Wowability.

(4) Low Importance for Consumers, High Score in Familiarity, and High Score in Exceeding Expectations

There are two strategies that the brand could employ in such a scenario. It could allocate fewer resources to the contact point, since consumers do not see it as important. Alternatively, it could add a spin to the contact point and turn it into a Point of Difference for the brand. If the brand is successful in portraying that contact point as special, it will raise the importance of that contact point in consumers' minds and increase the overall value of the brand.

(5) Low Importance for Consumers, Low Score in Familiarity, and Low Score in Exceeding Expectations

This contact point is one that consumers do not pay much attention to and do not know much about. Even though the brand is barely exceeding expectations in it, the brand might reasonably decide not to allocate more resources to improving it. Having said that, the brand should always be on the lookout for contact points whose importance to consumers can be enhanced, and which can be turned into Wow points.

Using these guidelines, the brand can formulate some preliminary strategies. For example, if one of the brand's contact points falls under category three and the brand knows that it has the budget to advertise, it can immediately proceed to rectify the problem. However, if the brand cannot immediately identify the best course of action, it could then apply the strategies that follow to narrow down the contact points to improve. The two approaches below allow the brand to choose an optimal and balanced set of contact points to focus on.

The first is an Outside-In approach where the thought process is consumer-centric. For this, the brand must create a list of contact points ranked by consumers in terms of importance. If consumers rank price as the most important contact point, the price performance of Brand A needs to be compared with that of its competitors. If Brand A is behind in price, then that is one of the contact points it needs to consider working on. If the brand is a leader in that contact point, it should maintain its performance in it, but also start paying attention to the next most important contact point on the list.

Similarly, if a contact point is important to consumers but they are unaware of it in a brand, the brand will have to find ways to increase consumers' familiarity with it. The brand may also have to improve its performance in that contact point. This is to ensure that once consumers become aware of the contact point, it will at least meet, and preferably exceed, their expectations.

The second approach takes a reverse Inside-Out point of view. This strips the brand down to its fundamentals and looks at the contact points that a brand is relatively strong in from a management perspective. The point is for the brand to keep doing what it is already good at. This strategy, as attractive as it may seem to managers, has its drawbacks. By being too inward looking, the brand runs the risk of missing out on shifts in consumer tastes. In the long run, it is still important to be consumer-centric in order to remain relevant to them.

Both the approaches should be used in tandem because they target certain strengths as well as weaknesses of a brand in the short and long term. Some contact points may overlap, and more attention should be paid to these as several approaches can be used concurrently to turn them into Wow points.

The desired outcome of using these approaches is to identify a set of key contact points that can be brought into the next stage where ideas on improving them are generated.

Tool 2: The Wowability Test

The Wowability Test identifies how well the brand is performing in the various contact points as compared to its competitors. This tool is structured as a quiz to be filled in by the people responsible for the brand. This could include anyone, ranging from the president of the company and the head of finance, to the sales staff. As with the Wow Score, this test can be customized to suit individual brands, but the general structure should be kept the same.

The strength of this tool lies in its succinctness and its ability to give results quickly. Although it cannot compare to feedback from a large group of consumers, the responses of an experienced brand manager can be extremely valuable.

The steps are listed below and the scores are tabulated at the end.

The Wowability Test

(1) List all relevant competitors.
(2) List the five contact points in this product category that are most important to consumers. Award five points to the most important contact point; four points to the second most important contact point, and so on.
(3) For the contact points listed in 2, name the top three brands for each contact point. Is your brand featured as a

relevant brand in these five contact points? Top brand = 5 points, Number 2 brand = 3 points, Number 3 brand = 1 point.

Compare 2 and 3. Are the five most important contact points for consumers the contact points that your brand excels at? If not, why?

Tabulate the scores using the formula (Importance of contact point X Position of brand for that contact point) to see where your brand stands on that contact point.

Table 8.2: Importance Table Template

Importance 5 = most important	Important Contact Points	Brand Number 1 (5 pts)	Brand Number 2 (3 pts)	Brand Number 3 (1 pt)
5				
4				
3				
2				
1				

Example of Using the Wowability Test

In this industry, there are five players (Brands A, B, C, D, and E) and advertising is the most important contact point for consumers, followed by packaging, customer service, price, and product quality. (Contact points here have been chosen at random.)

- For advertising, the top three brands are Brand A, Brand C, and Brand E.
- For packaging, the top three brands are Brand B, Brand A, and Brand C.
- For customer service, the top three brands are Brand A, Brand C, and Brand D.
- For price, the top three brands are Brand C, Brand D, and Brand B.
- For product quality, the top three brands are Brand D, Brand A, and Brand B.

Table 8.3: Example of Importance Table

Importance 5 =most important	Important contact points	Number One (5 pts)	Number Two (3 pts)	Number Three (1 pt)
5	Advertising	Brand A	Brand C	Brand E
4	Packaging	Brand B	Brand A	Brand C
3	Customer Service	Brand A	Brand C	Brand D
2	Price	Brand C	Brand D	Brand B
1	Product Quality	Brand D	Brand A	Brand B

Tabulation of the scores is as follows:

Table 8.4: Example of Tabulation of Scores

Contact points	Brands with Wow points				
	A	B	C	D	E
Advertising (5)	25	–	15	–	5
Packaging (4)	12	20	4	–	–
Customer Service (3)	15	–	9	3	–
Price (2)	–	2	10	6	–
Product Quality (1)	3	1	–	5	–
Total Score	55	23	38	14	5

The total scores (Maximum score: 75, minimum score: 0) are then compared with the ranges below for an idea of the brand's position in the market.

<u>60-75:</u> The brand is currently the dominant brand in the market. It has a virtual monopoly, and the company is enjoying the profits this position brings.

<u>45-59:</u> The brand is in a strong position and is most probably the market leader, but there may be one or two other brands close behind.

<u>30-44:</u> The brand is in a relatively good position, but more can be done to boost its market share. If the score is enough to make it the number one brand in the market, then the industry has a few major players jostling for leadership. Competition is fierce, and profit margins are likely to be narrow.

<u>15-29:</u> The brand needs to do more to turn its contact points into Wow points. It is ranked mostly second or third for all important contact points, or it may lead in the less important ones. Either way, this translates into mediocrity and a lack of focus.

<u>0-14:</u> The brand will suffer if there is no change to how it is perceived by consumers. The company should focus its efforts on turning its contact points into Wow points, starting with just one significant contact point. This will give it a boost in terms of market share, which will in turn motivate employees.

Once the company has decided on the contact points it wants to act on, its stakeholders can use the brainstorming techniques described in the next chapter to come up with ideas to turn them into Wow points. The results from the quiz can also be used to determine the brand's position on the FAR matrices. The brand can use these matrices to determine what its strategy needs to be.

The company should further identify three contact points, in addition to the five listed in Point 2, which may become important in the future. It should also identify current and upcoming trends. Brainstorming techniques can be used to try to ride these trends and capitalize on changing consumer behavior.

Limitations of the Wowability Test

As employees of the brand, there may be some bias toward it when taking this test. When the test is offered to a wide range of employees to be tabulated for senior management, employees may also feel obliged to name their brand as number one in categories where there is a high level of subjectivity. This problem can be avoided by making all responses anonymous. Make it clear that fair answers should be given based on respondents' own experiences with the brand, and what they have noticed in consumers and competitors..

Looking at the brand from within the company, meanwhile, may provide a view different from that of someone on the outside looking in (consumers).

There are also no ideal scores here. Instead, this test focuses on the overall positioning of the brand based on its most important contact points, and relative to its closest rivals.

How to Make Use of the Test Results

A brand can improve its positioning in the following ways:
(1) Improve its most important contact points.
(2) Make the contact points in which it is currently leading more important to consumers.
(3) Introduce new contact points that it can use to enhance its overall position.

This test is a tool that is highly economical, and brand managers should attempt to administer it on a regular basis in order to monitor the position of the brand. Although this test is useful, any disturbing patterns it picks up should be confirmed by a more thorough test, like the Wow Score survey. An example of a disturbing pattern would occur if competitors were mentioned more often than the brand as being relevant. In addition, if the brand is losing its place as the top performer in a particular contact point, this may indicate a problem that should be investigated.

Tool 3: The FAR Paradigm

The FAR Paradigm uses three dimensions to analyze how information affecting the brand's standing is processed by the consumer: Familiarity, Attractiveness, and Reputation.

The basic premise is that without these, consumers would not consider the brand. Chapter 2 on Brand Banking showed that brands need to increase their overall balance to improve their position on the consumer preference ladder. It established that a brand bank exists for brands that consumers are familiar with and that those banks consist of accounts that are regularly credited or debited. This is useful in helping to understand how the brands that consumers are familiar with are entered into their consideration set and ranked. Using brand banking, a brand can determine where it lies vis-à-vis the competition, and by how much it needs to improve in relation to them.

Familiarity—A Spectrum of Awareness Levels Pertaining to a Brand

Awareness is akin to the setting up of a brand bank in the consumer's mind. After the brand bank has been set up, further information that is banked about the brand will increase the consumer's familiarity. The stronger the awareness of the brand, the more likely it is that consumers will accrue information about it. In other words, information about a brand that is familiar to consumers is more likely to be registered in their consciousness.

Hence, it is crucial for a brand to increase consumers' familiarity with it because this allows better processing of any information that can increase the brand's bank balance. Familiarity also acts as a filter for the relevance and credibility of all information. Thus all information regarding the brand that is of no relevance or seems unbelievable to the consumer is flagged down.

More importantly, as familiarity increases, so does the possibility of trial. A consumer may not buy an unknown brand of apple juice, but if convinced to try the product—perhaps after learning that it is enriched with vitamin C and has extra fiber—she would be more likely to choose a brand that she is familiar with.

Familiarity is thus an important component in determining the success of a brand. It not only acts as a bridge between consumers and brands but also makes trial more likely.

Attractiveness—A Corollary of Wowability

For any brand, attractiveness is a necessity for it to be included in the consumer's consideration set, and ultimately be purchased. But it will only be placed at the top of the list if it achieves Wowability. In fact, Wowability is a sort of extreme attractiveness. Yet mere attractiveness is not what we are after, so as we discuss the matrices, we will use the term "Wowability" instead of attractiveness because Wowability is what we would like to achieve.

Reputation—Trustworthiness of a Brand

The reputation of a brand and the trust it inspires in consumers play an important role in building loyalty. Consumer loyalty is one of the larger goals of a brand because then the brand becomes more than the consumer's first choice. It becomes his only choice.

With trial and repeat purchases, consumers accrue experience with the brand, gaining satisfaction from the quality of its products. The brand establishes a relationship of trust with its consumers as it satisfies their needs and meets their expectations time and again.

Reputation forms a vault where every experience with the brand, and knowledge of other people's experiences with it, build up. A brand has to consistently deliver results for it to have a good reputation. Reputable brands tend to be near the top of the consumer's consideration set.

Relevance—the Necessary Catalyst

The FAR Paradigm shows that Familiarity, Attractiveness, and Reputation are necessary for a brand to improve its standing in consumers' minds. With these, the brand will be near the top of the consideration set when consumers are making purchase decisions.

Relevance is needed before a brand is even considered for inclusion in the consideration set. Relevance can arise from a variety of factors, including need satisfaction where the need could be real or perceived. Relevance drives the consumer toward the brand. Brands can also create relevance in consumers' minds. A brand like Coca-Cola may be impressive and score high on Familiarity, Attractiveness, and Reputation, but if a consumer is simply looking for bottled water, then Coca-Cola would not be in his consideration set. However, if this consumer is looking for something sweet and refreshing, Coca-Cola will probably be near the top of his consideration set. A brand should not attempt to be everything to everyone, because this dilutes its focus and may end up confusing consumers. Rather, a brand has to convey what its relevance is, so that its positioning is clear in the consumer's mind.

The FAR Paradigm as a Tool

The FAR Paradigm is used primarily to understand how brands are evaluated in the minds of consumers. Brands must first be familiar to consumers and then be attractive to them. Finally, brands have to develop a favorable reputation to gain their loyalty. FAR also shows how these dimensions affect consumer reaction. The effects are distilled below, in Figure 8.1.

Figure 8.1: FAR and Consumer Reaction

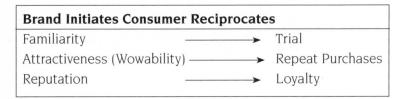

Brand Initiates Consumer Reciprocates	
Familiarity	Trial
Attractiveness (Wowability)	Repeat Purchases
Reputation	Loyalty

Brand managers need the FAR Paradigm to determine where the brand stands and then use the appropriate strategy to improve its standing.

Using the FAR Paradigm

Simply looking at the brand from a single dimension would not paint an insightful picture of it. For example, looking at the FAR Paradigm Familiarity Matrix below, low familiarity would not lead to high repeat purchases even if a brand has Wowability.

Charting a brand on the FAR Paradigm will produce two matrices, each mapping out two of the three dimensions. Brands can use the results from the Wow Score to determine their position on the FAR matrices. When the scores in the three dimensions—Familiarity, Attractiveness and Reputation—are low, the brand would be in the low square for each of these dimensions. An arbitrary cut-off point needs to be decided upon in order to be able to place the brand in the high or low square. Once the cut-off point has been decided upon, it should remain constant for all brands.

The main goal for brands is to be in Quadrant 1 of both matrices. Quadrant 4 signifies a brand in trouble. Brands falling in Quadrants 2 or 3 are in a moderate position, and need to improve in one dimension—be it Familiarity, Attractiveness or Reputation—to allow them to cross over to Quadrant 1. A brand in Quadrant 1 for all three dimensions is likely to be the market leader and the brand that others emulate.

FAR Paradigm Familiarity Matrix

Figure 8.2: Familiarity-Wowability Matrix

	Low Familiarity	High Familiarity
Wowability	Unclaimed Potential **II**	High Repeat Purchases **I**
No Wowability	Tough Square **IV**	Maybe Square **III**

Tough Square

Every brand starts out in the Tough square, where familiarity with the product is low and there are obstacles preventing repeat purchases, like pricing or start-up problems. The brand has two objectives at this point: to create Wowability and to increase Familiarity among its intended customers. It is recommended that the brand tackle these two objectives simultaneously because without Familiarity, a brand that has Wowability cannot profit from it, and without Wowability, an increase in Familiarity will not result in consumers switching to this new brand.

Maybe Square

Looking at the two objectives mentioned above, it is easier for a brand to increase Familiarity than create Wowability. Increasing Familiarity involves increasing consumer contact with the brand, possibly through advertising. It requires setting up the brand bank, and activating it so that consumers will be reminded of the brand in their daily lives. Once consumers are familiar with the brand, they may be willing to try its products. However, if the brand does not have Wowability, consumers may not buy its products again, leading to high customer turnover and low sales. Brands that fall into this category tend to be newer names that have advertised heavily to introduce themselves to consumers, but may have very little to offer them in terms of Wowability. They fall into the Maybe square, brands that consumers may or may not choose.

Unclaimed Potential Square

When there is Wowability and low Familiarity, the brand has a few options. Customers are generally not familiar with it, but those that are and have tried its product have had their expectations exceeded. Companies that fall into this category tend to be small outfits that offer high-quality products and services, but which do not promote their products for reasons, such as budget constraints. Their sales are low, but customer turnover is also low. If the company wants to expand, it will need to make its brand familiar to a wider audience, and this may lead to a surge in sales, moving the brand to the High Repeat Purchases square if it is able to maintain its standards.

High Repeat Purchases Square

When there is Wowability and high Familiarity, the brand enjoys a high number of repeat purchases. Customers are familiar with the brand, and their expectations are consistently exceeded by it. Having established a strong foundation, the brand can now move on to Matrix 2.

FAR Paradigm Reputation Matrix

Figure 8.3: Wowability—Reputation Matrix

	No Wowability	Wowability
High Reputation	Problem Square III	Loyal Users I
Low Reputation	Tough Square IV	Maybe Repeat Purchasers II

Tough Square

Brands in the Tough square have no Wowability and low Reputation. This means that they do not feature high in the consideration set of customers and tend to be unappealing. Brands in this category include failing brands or very new brands. These brands need to go back to the Familiarity Matrix and reexamine their position. If they scored low on Familiarity, then they will need to intensify their advertising efforts. If they scored high on Familiarity, then the main challenge lies in creating Wowability to encourage repeat purchases. From there, the brand can move to the Repeat Purchases square.

Problem Square

Brands in the Problem square score high on Reputation, but have no Wowability. Brands in this category are mainly well-known brands that have made mistakes, leading to a decrease in Wowability. Brands that fall into the Problem square have the luxury of having a good Reputation, which means that if they act quickly to recover their Wowability, they can still rise to the Loyal Users square.

Maybe Repeat Purchases Square

Compared to the Problem square, brands that fall in this square have a more difficult task: to build their Reputation. That means the company has to continue doing everything it has done to reach this square, and then do more to improve its status with consumers. In short, the brand needs to sustain its Wowability now that the foundation has been laid. This is akin to trying to climb up an escalator that is moving down. It will be harder to delight consumers now that the brand has shown that it can deliver more. But if this is achieved, its Reputation will be solidly established.

Loyal Users Square

Brands in this square enjoy low customer turnover and are usually market leaders. Their customers place them first in their consideration set, and they are not easily displaced due to the strong emotions consumers have towards them. These brands have the privilege of being part of consumers' lives in return for not having disappointed them.

Putting it All Together

By rethinking how brands are perceived, companies can be more focused and effective in targeting contact points that are important to consumers. The aim is to increase the amount of positive information consumers receive about the brand. By using the FAR Paradigm matrices, brands can focus their resources on improving their position in the areas they are weak in, using the strategies discussed. This approach prevents them from overdirecting resources toward their strengths and focuses on eliminating their weaknesses and minimizes the wastage of limited resources.

The FAR paradigm is based on the results of the Wow Score survey, which requires a relatively large pool of respondents to ensure maximum reliability. Despite the effort required, both the survey and the Wowability Test remain extremely helpful in pinpointing the areas where brands need to focus, even more so when used together.

Ultimately the opinions of consumers are key, because brands survive based on how consumers take to them.

!

"Branding demands
commitment; commitment
to continual re-invention;
striking chords with people
to stir their emotions;
and commitment to
imagination. It is easy
to be cynical about such
things, much harder
to be successful."[1]

— Richard Branson, CEO of Virgin Enterprises

chapter 9

Laddering, brainstorming, and mind mapping are qualitative tools that can be used in tandem with the quantitative tools discussed in Chapter 8 in the quest for Wowability.

Laddering

Laddering[2] is a form of questioning that allows researchers to delve deeper and deeper into the consumer psyche. It discovers which attributes of a product have meaningful associations for the consumer by peeling away superficial answers to arrive at the deeper need that any brand, product, or contact point satisfies.

The simplest line of questioning would determine the following:

- Which important contact point distinguishes a brand from its competitors?
- Which brand is preferred overall, and what it is about its key contact point that makes it so appealing to the consumer?
- Why such qualities are important to the consumer?

Although people do buy products to satisfy their physical needs, when choosing between brands, a preference for a particular contact point often indicates an emotional need. Laddering can analyze a brand's contact points by looking at the fundamental psychological needs that these contact points satisfy.

Laddering is also a fairly quick method to determine which contact points need to be turned into Wow points for the brand. It does not require a large sample to establish certain truths about the appeal of a brand. Interviewing a group of around 20 consumers is likely to result in answers that are remarkably similar although these consumers may lead very different lives. This technique supplements the surveys discussed in Chapter 8, providing brands with greater insight into the emotional needs that its contact points can satisfy. Knowing that consumers are seeking to satisfy a particular need allows the brand to look for viable ways to fill that need.

Brainstorming

The concept of "brainstorming" was coined by Alex Faickney Osborn, co-founder of the BBDO ad agency, in late 1939.[3] He described brainstorming as "a creative technique of generating ideas to solve a problem."[4]

It can be done individually, although it is more commonly used and more effective in a group. The main goal of brainstorming is to generate as many ideas as possible. These ideas often trigger others, resulting in a stream of ideas.

Many assume that brainstorming involves a fairly informal gathering of people discussing a problem and trying to come up with the perfect solution. Yet, without adhering to a set of guidelines, discussion may waste time and not yield any appreciable results.

Osborn's classic *Your Creative Power*[5] extolled the virtues of brainstorming and the basic guidelines, or rules, that he suggested in it still apply today.[6] They are:

- No criticism
- Quantity over quality
- Any idea is welcomed
- Bounce ideas off each other to create new ideas

Using these simple rules, a group of people can discuss a problem and seek an optimal solution. This generation of solutions and process of ideation is brainstorming. The goal is to create a large pool of ideas that can be later filtered and synthesized to eventually arrive at a workable solution. Once a few contact points have been short-listed, brainstorming techniques can be used to figure out ways to turn them into Wow points.

IBM's Wow Story

IBM took the concept of brainstorming to its limits with Innovation Jam. Employees and their families, customers, and consultants were invited to two- or three-day online events focused on applying IBM's technology to areas like transportation, health, environment, finance, and commerce.[7] The conventional view of a brainstorm is that the more participants you have, the harder it is to control, and you can end up with groupthink and social loafing. IBM's Innovation Jam involved more than 150,000 people from 104 countries,[8] but the company did not face significant problems. This was largely because the issues discussed were generally those that affected everyone. With an online platform, every idea could be properly stored and opened for discussion in a systematic way. This is similar to the internet forums. IBM employees threw conversation starters into the ring, and the participants offered suggestions on future technology that could solve these problems.

Since 2001, IBM has hosted collaborative forums on innovation for its employees. The company also regularly hosts a Global Innovation Outlook process, where hundreds of organizations gather to discuss business and societal innovation opportunities. To underscore the importance of brainstorming to the company, CEO Sam Palmisano promised $100 million[9] toward bringing the best ideas to fruition. IBM later funded ten of the best ideas that emerged from these sessions, including a 3D internet, branchless banking, and a system that creates more environmentally friendly business solutions.[10]

Common Misconceptions About Brainstorming

The advantages of brainstorming as a means of generating ideas are obvious. However, companies often give up on it when it does not produce the expected results. As useful as brainstorming can be, it requires patience and perseverance to arrive at a solution.

Myth #1: Brainstorming will provide a quick solution

Brainstorming may seem easy, but it takes time and practice to achieve results. Each participant has to be sufficiently prepared for the session, and the facilitator must be sufficiently experienced to allow everyone a chance to contribute while keeping the session focused. A common misconception of brainstorming is that it is like taking a painkiller—it provides fast relief. Unfortunately, this is not the case.

Myth #2: Brainstorming needs a creative ideas person

There is no such thing as a creative ideas person, or someone who can provide the best solution every time. It is imperative for the team to believe that the best ideas will not come from a single source, but rather be an amalgamation of ideas that come together into a coherent, credible solution. This is crucial if the brainstorming process is to turn out the most useful ideas. Everyone needs to pull her own weight by suggesting an idea, or taking someone else's idea in a new direction to produce a pool much larger than what any single person could have developed.

Myth #3: There is no need to define the problem at hand

How would you like to try to solve a problem without actually knowing what it is? The very first thing the facilitator needs to do is define the problem at hand. Asking the right question is crucial. Are sales going down, or do they only appear to be going down because a smaller crowd was seen during a particular weekend? The team would first need to gather sales data and compare this with previous records. Check the news for anything that may be related to the dip. For example, banks may have increased interest rates. Perhaps there was an accident near the mall causing drivers and their families to divert to another part of the city. Consider the two questions: "How do we increase sales?" and "How do we increase sales to first-time homebuyers in light of the mortgage rate hike?" The latter is more specific, allowing team members to focus their thoughts on a specific issue and come up with a better solution.

Myth #4: There is no need to prepare for brainstorming sessions

Nobody should walk into a brainstorming session unprepared. Each team member should do basic research so that ideas generated at the session take into account potential pitfalls. Team members would also be more aware of the viability of the ideas that are generated if they have prepared in advance. People brainstorming ideas to improve a drive-through service, for example, may make it a point to actually experience the service themselves. They can use the opportunity to take note of any shortcomings that they would not have otherwise known about. Other forms of research could include trying out competing drive-through services so that any desirable facets can be replicated to enhance the experience for consumers.

Myth #5: Brainstorming gives the perfect solution every time

A big caveat of brainstorming is that it does not guarantee immediate and perfect solutions every time. Brainstorming works best for achieving incremental progress: for example, how the brand can increase customer satisfaction levels during the next holiday season. This is more practical than asking "How can we become the nation's top brand for customer service?" A single brainstorming session would not be nearly enough for tackling such a large issue.

Instead, the company's management will need to examine the level of customer service it currently provides, and then use brainstorming to find ways to improve each aspect, like pre- or post-purchase service, delivery and so on. Because it is conceptual in nature, a broad question like "How do we become the market leader?" may be hard to answer using brainstorming. On the other hand, dividing the question into smaller sub-questions could yield impressive results. For an automobile manufacturer, the question "How do we become the market leader?" can be broken into sub-questions like "How can we improve the interior or exterior design of this car?" or "What colors will be popular in the future?" or even "What kind of cup holder would work with this model?" Breaking down the larger question into smaller questions may suggest possible Wow points that the company can focus on.

Mind Mapping

"The Mind Map is an expression of Radiant Thinking and is therefore a natural function of the human mind. It is a powerful graphic technique which provides a universal key to unlocking the potential of the brain."[11]

– Tony Buzan, *The Mind Map Book.*

A mind map is a graphic representation of a network of ideas, tasks, and keywords that is centered on a main idea. To begin, put the subject or the issue squarely in the middle of a page using just a keyword to represent it. Avoid using phrases because focus may be placed, quite inappropriately, on the other words. Take, for example, a brand manager for Ferrari looking to come up with a strategy to launch the Modena 360. The keyword to use would be the name of the car, rather than a phrase like "Strategy for the launch of Modena 360." If the whole phrase is used, the focus may blur because of the word "strategy" or "launch," neglecting the car itself. Drawings can be used interchangeably with words. Each line radiating from the keyword should have only one word (or drawing) at the end of it. So if there are five issues regarding the launch of the Modena 360, then there should only be five lines leading from Modena 360 to the five issues, each represented by a keyword or drawing. More ideas will in turn radiate out from each of these five issues. In a mind map, all lines should be connected such that every idea can be traced back to the keyword. There should never be lines hanging out of nowhere, or it will be difficult to tell where the idea originated, especially when looking at the mind map after time has passed.

Mind mapping is useful as it lays out our thoughts in a visual format, allowing us to view the problem in an organized way. Having a visual display also lets us look at the problem more clearly and immediately identify areas where there are fewer ideas.

Simply writing ideas down as a list will not allow us to see that we have a balanced quantity of ideas for each section as easily as a mind map does. Also, part of the power of mind maps lies in the way the links between words and concepts are clearly shown by lines and arrows. Sometimes, one can even see how some keywords are common to different roots.

3M's Wow Story

"Management that is destructively critical when mistakes are made kills initiative. It's essential that we have many people with initiative if we are to continue to grow."

– William L. McKnight, Former President and Chairman of 3M[12]

Innovation and coming up with creative new ideas are assumed to be the prerogative of young and small companies that have a lot of maneuverability. At over one hundred years old and pulling in an estimated $22.9 billion in revenue in 2006,[13] 3M is neither. While other companies similar in size and age tend to adopt a more parochial attitude, 3M is recognized for its innovation. By exceeding the expectations that consumers have, its products have consistently impressed. While 3M's products are definitely of high quality, its Wowability lies in its penchant for creating products that satisfy needs consumers do not even realize they have.

If you are a student or if you work in an office, you would have used a Post-it. You are probably unable to imagine working without them. However, before 3M created them, few would have believed that they would need small scraps of paper with low adhesive at the back. Thus, when 3M came up with the Post-it, it far exceeded expectations. Leaving notes became so much easier, and consumers gradually found other uses for the Post-it. Although the formulation of the low adhesive was an accident, only an innovative company would have found a use for it.

The Post-it is still evolving. In 2006, 3M introduced its latest invention, Post-it Picture Paper.[14] As the name suggests, pictures can now be printed at home on special 3M paper and immediately stuck on the fridge, wall, or any other space. The company is currently developing "stickable" index cards and is continuing to look for new ways to extend the Post-it line.

In 2006, 3M placed third in *BusinessWeek's* rankings of the world's most innovative companies. According to the company, seven main factors have allowed it to maintain innovation as a key Wow point:[15]

1. It is dedicated to innovation; in 2005 it spent $1.24 billion on research and development aimed at creating new products.
2. Its corporate culture is in tune with its goal to keep innovating; it hires employees who are creative and pioneers.
3. It focuses on technology and ensures that it has the newest tools to create new products.
4. It encourages networking within the organization so that thoughts, ideas, and even problems are shared.
5. It rewards employees for exceptional work, awarding outstanding achievers and their families holidays at 3M resorts.
6. It always quantifies its efforts.
7. It ensures that research is tied to the consumer and that the products it makes are in line with what the consumer needs.

3M also has a system in place to track the rate of innovation at the company. Its management regularly examines sales figures to ensure that the company earns a healthy portion of its revenue from new products. This forces it to innovate rather than simply improve on existing product lines.

Motorola's Wow Story

Motorola embraced change with the creation of the Razr, a design clearly different from and superior to anything it had produced before. The fact that the Razr was the slimmest phone on the market at the time of its 2004[16] launch, and still managed to provide all standard functions, exceeded consumer expectations.

In order to develop a new and innovative product in the intensely competitive cell phone market, the Motorola team knew that it had to design something that was not only aesthetically different, but also highly functional.

From the very beginning, Motorola ensured that it had a firm grasp on what consumers wanted. The company conducted research to discover which hand phone features consumers liked and which they disliked. Motorola concluded that consumers preferred flip phones.[17] However, the fact that such phones were bulky when closed was a primary concern. Hence, Motorola focused its efforts on creating a sleek and slim hand phone that could be folded. It was a struggle to develop technology thin enough to support the design of the phone, but Motorola engineers finally came up with a unique product that Wowed consumers.

The chief of marketing for the Razr project, Geoffrey Frost, was glued to the idea of creating a truly memorable product that would have a competitive edge over other hand phones on the market. Guidelines and goals for the production of the Motorola Razr were all aimed at ensuring Wowability. Core principles required team members to instill Wowability into the newly developed phone. These components were surprise, honesty, richness, and simplicity.[18] These qualities were singled out as the ones that would produce a hand phone that would excel as well as be unique. Not only were there internal expectations that had to be met, such as critical completion dates and specific performance standards, but other distinct goals, such as the "three-meter rule," were also set. This rule is particularly interesting, since its main objective was to make the model so unique that it could be identified from 10 feet away.

Beyond product functionality and design, other strategies were also put in place. One unique strategy initiated by Frost was to market the Razr through product placement. The Razr was placed in popular television shows, such as *The Sopranos*. In one episode, lead character Tony Soprano commented that "Motorola's supposed to be the best."[19] This type of publicity greatly benefited the brand. When consumers saw the product on their favorite television shows, it exceeded their expectations.

!

"Innovation is not absolutely necessary, but then, neither is survival!"[1]

— Andrew Papageorge, Founder of GoInnovate!

chapter 10

You can sustain Wowability in two broad ways: by increasing total value so that it stays above consumer expectations, or by managing consumer expectations so that it is easier to maintain total value above it. Countries manage GDP expectations by periodically announcing projections for both the key figure and the economic indicators contributing to it. This has the effect of softening any blows as compared to countries that give no indication about their economic performance, and then drop a nasty surprise when the GDP figure shows a slowdown. Public companies do the same thing, issuing profit warnings to lower investor expectations. They may even claim a small victory if the results are not as bad as anticipated.

Ever-Increasing Consumer Expectations

Singapore Airlines is widely regarded as one of the best airlines in the world, winning numerous accolades each year. Excellent service is one of its hallmarks, and the company works hard to maintain this Wow point. One of the constant struggles for Singapore Airlines is keeping up with the high expectations customers have when they board its planes. Passengers expect more from the service, the food, and the onboard entertainment on Singapore Airlines than they do of any other airline. Even if Singapore Airlines continues to strive to provide better experiences for its customers, the incremental improvements will decrease over time. This could happen for a variety of reasons: 1) The "easy" contact points may have already been converted into Wow points; 2) Competitors are copying any innovation that Singapore Airlines makes, eroding its Wowability; or 3) Consumer expectations have grown faster than the airline's ability to increase total value. These issues are common to most industries. So how does a company manage rising expectations?

Managing Expectations by Managing Release Dates

When Airbus first unveiled the A380 in January 2005,[2] it was hailed as the next step in aviation. The A380 would be the first aircraft with the capacity to carry up to 800 passengers. The market could only support one manufacturer in this niche, and so Airbus had been keen to introduce its aircraft ahead of competitor Boeing. Airbus thus achieved Wowability by exceeding existing expectations. It had identified which contact points it needed to improve on and had also, presumably, thought about exactly what changes it had to make to increase the overall value of its brand.

The plan was well thought through, and the strategy seemed sound. In June 2005, however, Airbus announced its first delay. Singapore Airlines was now to receive the world's first A380 in the last quarter of 2006. By June 2006, Airbus had announced a second delay, and this time, the delivery date was pushed back a further six months. Cost overruns and compensation to airlines for late deliveries resulted in a loss of $3.6 billion in earnings.[3] In the wake of the second delay, EADS, which owns 80% of Airbus, saw its share price fall 26%, and its CEO Noël Forgeard, along with Airbus CEO Gustav Humbert and A380 Program Manager Charles Champion, tendered their resignations.[4]

What went wrong with the A380? The French and German Airbus plants did not update each other on changes made to key aircraft parts, and when the changed parts arrived in Toulouse to be assembled, the inevitable happened: They did not fit.[5] For Airbus, the cost of raising expectations but failing to meet, much less exceed them, is likely to total upwards of $6.1 billion by 2010.[6]

On the other hand, the predictable rate at which each new generation of the iPod hits the market allows consumer expectations to be expertly managed by brand owner Apple. Imagine if the company did not regulate these release dates. It would confuse consumers if the latest versions hit the market in very quick succession and would result in impatience and disappointment if the wait was longer than anticipated.

The timeline in Figure 10.1 shows that Apple releases updated versions of its iPod (at the top of the diagram) about once a year. With each release, new features are added and memory capacity is beefed up. iPod's most recent version, the iPod Classic, which was released in September 2007 and comes with storage space of 80GB or 160GB,[8] is able to store both music and videos, and boasts a radio feature for podcasts. The 160 GB iPod can store up to 40,000 songs. Apple ensures that it continues to exceed consumer expectations and that consumers buy the latest iPod. The same strategy is employed for the iPod Nano and iPod Shuffle, with release dates spaced

Figure 10.1: iPod Release Timeline[7]

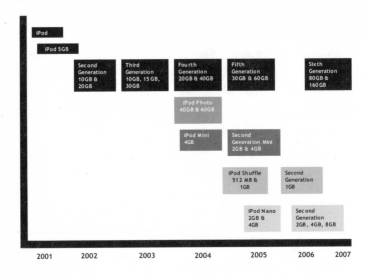

about a year apart. Because Apple has three different kinds of iPods rolling out each year, consumers are constantly introduced to newer versions, allowing expectations to grow at a manageable pace. This way iPod's Wowability does not fizzle out, and Apple can get more mileage out of the newer versions and the iPod brand overall.

Barriers to Wowability

Although it would be ideal to set up barriers preventing competitors from attaining Wowability, this is much easier said than done. Yet, once you have achieved Wowability, you must try to prevent competitors from simply imitating you and creating the same value you provide. You can be sure that if the Wow point you create is easy to reproduce, your competitors will adopt it. In a world of advanced technology, reverse engineering can imitate more and more technical innovations. Although patent laws protect innovations, very often the application process—and the judicial process when an infringement occurs—takes too long to be effective. This problem is exacerbated in developing countries where counterfeiting is rife and intellectual property laws are not strictly adhered to. This is another reason why Wowability and brand loyalty are crucial.

Functional Contact Points

Functional contact points, like memory capacity and price, are especially vulnerable to imitation. Suppose our brand of notebook computers, Brand X, comes up with a line of notebooks that have the highest memory capacity available in the market, say 120 gigabytes. People who are Wowed by this would buy it, but a few months later, some of Brand X's biggest competitors are likely to come up with notebooks with even better specifications, with 128 gigabytes of memory, for example. The Wowability of Brand X would then vanish quickly. Functional Wow points are the hardest to protect against imitation and to create barriers to. This ease of entry is especially noticeable in the retail industry. Although illegal, many manufacturers produce imitations of branded luxury goods. It is not uncommon to see an imitation Prada handbag in a Thai night market for one-sixteenth of the price of a real Prada bag. The functional characteristics in these cases are almost identical to the untrained eye.

Emotional Contact Points

Emotional contact points are also vulnerable to imitation, but to a much lower degree than functional contact points. Contact points like customer service are notoriously hard to imitate. How do you get a typical hotel's employees to behave like Four Seasons' employees? Brands with fantastic customer service often have a culture that encourages employees to behave the way they do. If a company does not have that kind of culture, it is a tall order indeed to imitate such a high level of service for a sustained period of time. Also, Wow points like design, advertising, and user experience are very often hard to imitate because it takes a high amount of creativity and ingenuity, as well as key insights to create Wow points out of these contact points. Thus, creating Wow points of a brand's emotional contact points should be emphasized.

Barriers to Entry

Apart from preventing existing competitors from copying your brand's Wow points, it is also important to prevent new players from easily entering your market. Part of preventing these players from encroaching into your turf is making sure your Wow points are difficult to imitate, and keeping track of under-exploited opportunities in the market. Consider expanding into these untapped niches by creating new brands if you want to avoid diluting your main brand.

Disruptive Wowability

An element of disruptive Wowability is similar to disruptive technologies,[9] or industry-changing technology. An example would be how transportation evolved from steamships to steam-powered trains, and then, the airplane.[10] Consumers still satisfied their need to get from one place to another, but as each new technology was invented, travel time decreased, resulting in increased value with each change. Disruptive Wowability is created from disruptive Wow points, which are more than just disruptive technologies. They include innovation in business models and processes, among other things, for example, Wal-Mart's ability to offer a wide variety of consumer goods at impossibly low prices. Look at how the small mom-and-pop stores are disappearing in neighborhoods where a Wal-Mart has been built. How about Dell's direct selling? Prices of PCs dropped, and competitors bled while Dell grew from strength to strength, overtaking companies like IBM, HP, and Lenovo to become the market leader. In 2005, Dell claimed 18.1% of the PC market compared with HP's 15.6% and Lenovo's 6.2%.[11] Toyota's efficient manufacturing process, iPod's design, and Ikea's fun and low-cost furniture retailing all transformed their industries and left many competing brands, big and small, behind in their wake.

Disruptive Wowability—Embrace it!

Figure 10.2 is an illustration of a brand that has continually created disruptive Wowability. Brands that fit into this mold include Apple, IBM, and General Electric. All have created industry-revolutionizing products. A company that does not aim to create disruptive Wowability in the long term is headed for failure, while a company that constantly seeks to exceed expectations will not only last, but also lead its sector. Of course, depending on the industry, the life expectancy of companies will differ. For example, General Electric and Sony both have a wide portfolio of businesses that are quite independent of each other. As long as they continue to use their vast resources to invent and embrace

Figure 10.2: Brand with multiple disruptive Wow points in its Wowability cycle

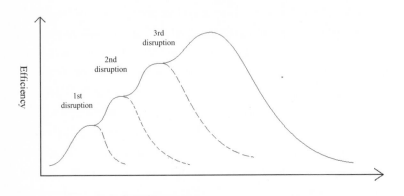

Exceeding Expectations

the latest technology, they will remain relevant. Companies in danger of becoming irrelevant are those who do not innovate. Let's say that there is now a new form of transportation that costs less, reduces travel time, and allows travelers to go anywhere they want safely. Airlines, no matter how much they try to stay ahead, will be at risk of becoming obsolete. They will have suddenly found themselves dealing with something completely unfamiliar, and if they do not exceed the expectations that consumers now have (set by the company that pioneered the new technology), they face the possibility of becoming mediocre and being driven out of business.

Incumbent market leaders face the dilemma of relying on what's familiar to them versus what could potentially change the market. These companies have a valuable advantage over industry newcomers in that they know what consumers value. However, a clear distinction must be made between knowing what consumers really want and what companies assume they want. When low-cost carriers entered the airlines industry, established airlines did not believe passengers would be willing to tolerate the low level of service, lack of amenities, and smaller planes in exchange for a cheaper ticket. Yet once they took off, the major airlines were forced to launch their own low-cost players to compete for a slice of the budget market.

Three companies that have successfully sustained their Wowability are General Electric, whose broad portfolio of businesses has evolved over the years alongside the changing technological landscape; Coca-Cola, which has stuck to its core product from the day of its inception back in 1886;[12] and Singapore Airlines, which has won more awards and achieved more recognition in the last few decades than most airlines have in a lifetime. Beyond the three companies, let's also take a look at a country—Singapore—that has done an amazing job of achieving and sustaining Wowability.

General Electric's Wow Story

Prior to the 1980s, many of General Electric's businesses dealt with infrastructure and other large-scale industrial engineering projects. The rate at which their products became obsolete was relatively slower than at companies like General Motors, thus GE was quite complacent. When Jack Welch took over in 1981, however, he demanded that GE's various businesses either be counted among the top two in their respective industries, or face being axed from the company.

One of the effects this had was to make the businesses more aware of emerging technology, since this had the potential to help them gain Wowability, hence propelling them to the number one slot or, if they were already there, blowing the competition off the map. The takeover of RCA (Radio Corporation of America) in 1986 marked another phase in GE's history. It was the first time the company grew through acquisition.[13] Welch understood that it would take too long for GE to grow a television network of its own, and the television programming industry was also not an area in which GE had any expertise. Its acquisition of RCA marked the start of a willingness to acquire good companies in order to establish a foothold in new industries. Getting rid of old, established mindsets was what Welch did in his quest to grow GE further. Another crucial element Welch brought to GE was the belief that "…someone, somewhere, has a better idea."[14] Learning from anyone, including those outside the company, was encouraged, and this helped to create an openness to ideas, another element that allowed GE to grow. Welch himself said that if he were the only one supplying ideas to GE, "it would only take an hour for it to sink." This openness allowed GE to embrace all forms of innovation, be it new technology or a new way to manage the business. The receptiveness to change and the determination to achieve market leadership created a hungry and flexible organization. Ironically, even as Welch tried to grow GE, he was equally focused on keeping it small. A small company has many advantages over big, lumbering giants. In fact, small companies are often the ones to develop industry-changing disruptions. When companies are at the top for too long and there are no legitimate competitors on the horizon, they grow complacent and may even ignore the customer. Smaller firms, on the other hand, work hard to maintain the smaller customer base that they have, and are hungry for more business. They also tend to be nimbler in decision making and have a bigger appetite for risk than larger companies. This is the perfect recipe for disruptive Wowability.

GE also ensured that it did not lose touch with its consumers, conducting regular meetings to ascertain that the brand continued to be relevant to them. The success the company enjoys today speaks for itself. With a culture that is open to better ideas and has a passion to excel, GE is on track to sustaining its Wowability for a long time to come.

Coca-Cola's Wow Story

Coca-Cola is rated as the number one brand in the world with an estimated value of US$67 billion.[15] Throughout its history, the company has worked to remain relevant to its consumers. This is no mean feat, considering how much society has changed since 1886. Although we have emphasized the benefits of sustaining Wowability by creating disruptive Wow points, Coca-Cola's experience has shown that not all planned disruptions are successful. In 1985, the cola giant launched a massive disaster: New Coke—a sweeter version meant to replace its flagship drink. Extensive market research had shown that a slight majority of consumers preferred the taste of Pepsi-Cola. Pepsi was fast catching up in terms of market share, and while still at the top, Coca-Cola felt it had to do something. The development of New Coke was perfectly sound; yet, it didn't work.

Coca-Cola's history is deeply intertwined with the history of the U.S., and as one consumer put it, "Changing Coke is like God making the grass purple."[16] What do you do when your brand is the generic brand for the category? When a brand has been the number one brand for a very long time, as Coca-Cola has, it is no longer just another consumer good. It becomes a cultural icon, a symbol of the nation even. This increases the risks of missteps like New Coke. Unlike technology, where the emphasis is on functional contact points, brands like Coca-Cola and McDonald's are dealing mostly with emotional contact points. Whereas GE was able to adapt to bring more functional value to its consumers, Coca-Cola provides very little functional value, but a lot of emotional value. When Coca-Cola changed its formula, this emotional relationship was affected, and consumers felt betrayed.

To sustain its Wowability, Coca-Cola should not concentrate on changing a subjective contact point like taste. It has already established itself as the front-running cola. All new cola drinks are benchmarked against Coca-Cola, and just as grass is supposed to be green, colas are supposed to taste like Coca-Cola. Today, Coca-Cola has several different versions on the market, but its flagship remains the original Coca-Cola. As it should.

Singapore Airlines' Wow Story

The airline industry possesses an extensive number of contact points. The largest chunk of an airline company's capital goes into the leasing, maintenance, and operation of planes, which provide the core functional value of transportation. Yet it is the sum of several seemingly small contact points that make a big difference to passengers. Singapore Airlines (SIA) has successfully exceeded expectations in most of these contact points and achieved Wowability. More important, it strives to sustain its Wowability to ensure that it remains the preferred airline for its customers.

SIA's Wowability began almost with its formation. It was one of the first airlines in the region with up-to-date jet airplanes, and its passenger service was remarkable. Its flight stewardesses, also known as the Singapore Girls, were exceptionally helpful. Thousands of customers have relayed stories about how the Singapore Girl went out of her way to help passengers and make their trip as pleasant as possible. By helping passengers beyond what was required of them in their capacity as flight attendants, the Singapore Girls exceeded expectations. Although SIA was able to garner Wowability early on, its tremendous success is due to its ability to sustain it. The brand has continued to add to its value and improve its service despite already being one of the best airlines globally.

SIA realized early on that "quality of service" was a key contact point. It works hard to ensure that its passengers across all classes are as comfortable as possible. Years ago, it became the first airline to offer free headsets and drinks to all its passengers.[17]

In addition, SIA also offers one of the best in-flight entertainment systems in the air. It far exceeded expectations when it began to offer economy class passengers individual TV screens. While other airlines were content to provide just one large screen for all passengers, SIA was willing to commit resources to offer passengers personalized entertainment. It could have simply chosen to offer newer releases, for example, and that would have added value without incurring as much cost. But SIA's willingness to go further than required has allowed it to increase and sustain its Wowability.

At the same time, SIA has also increased the amount of entertainment that passengers can receive from the system. Passengers of SIA have over 600 entertainment options, ranging from movies and television shows, to games and audio programs. This is the largest selection in the industry, and giving passengers this choice has turned SIA's in-flight entertainment into a Wow point.

This proactive approach was taken again when SIA refurbished its first class with seats that reclined 180 degrees into a flat bed.[18] This offered optimum comfort to passengers travelling longer distances. Each first class passenger was also provided with a 23-inch LCD screen[19] for one of the best viewing experiences in the sky.

There have been other improvements to SIA's first class cabin, but the key point here is that SIA is proactive in finding ways to exceed expectations, hence allowing it to sustain its Wowability. Its efforts mean that SIA is often the first choice of passengers, and have also translated into a 5-star rating by Skytrax, an independent airline research organization. SIA was one of only five airlines to have achieved this rating in 2007.[20]

Singapore's Wow Story

The history of Singapore is your typical rags to riches story. Just a few decades ago, it was a poor country that not many felt would make it. But not only has Singapore become a developed nation, it has also become a brand imbued with Wowability. It has consistently exceeded expectations, including, in the early days, those regarding its survival.

When Singapore separated from Malaysia in 1965,[21] it found itself quite helpless, since it did not have many natural resources or much experience at self-rule. Although today one could say that Singapore's greatest resource is its people, in 1963, unemployment was a serious issue. Reducing unemployment required training its populace and enhancing the overall economy. The Economic Development Board (EDB) was set up with its primary role to attract foreign investment to enhance the economy. Between 1971 and 1976, it opened offices in Zurich, Paris, Osaka, and several other key cities in the world.[22]

This had a two-fold effect: The EDB was able to learn about and address investor concerns, even as its physical presence acted as a communicational contact point, enhancing Singapore's value overseas and assuring potential investors that the city-state was absolutely serious about attracting foreign investment. Although common sense today, at that time, this strategy was quite revolutionary, especially coming from a small Southeast Asian nation. The strategy worked, and Singapore began chalking up more Wow points, but it did not stop there. It continued to add value to its "brand."

For example, Singapore ensured that its people had the technical skills and knowledge to contribute to the industrialization of the island and to provide a viable workforce for investors. Technical education was offered in secondary schools, and specialized training institutes were set up to equip workers with the necessary skills. This strategy added functional value to the brand and exceeded expectations as few nations at that time were dedicated enough to commit to such a large and long-term program. The quality of the workforce definitely exceeded investors' expectations and delighted them, creating Wowability for the Singapore brand in their minds.

Since then, Singapore has continued to sustain its Wowability. Despite its small size, the city-state was ranked 17th in terms of per capita GDP by the International Monetary Fund in 2006.[23] Its airport is renowned and ranked number one in the world[24] by the Airports International Council. Singapore is also home to the world's busiest port.[25] Beyond attracting investors, Singapore has also achieved Wowability in the eyes of its other target audiences, including its citizens, tourists, immigrants, and expatriate workers. Although not a conventional brand, Singapore has exceeded expectations, delighted its audiences, and achieved Wowability.

!

"What we call results are beginnings."[1]

– Ralph Waldo Emerson (1803 -1882), American author, poet, and philosopher

chapter 11

Let's conclude by taking a look at the general principles of Wowability.

Principle 1: Wowability Leads to First Preference

A brand that consistently delights by exceeding expectations has Wowability. And a brand that has Wowability is the first choice of its target audience. All brands should aspire to Wowability, and once they have achieved it, they should sustain it for as long as they can.

Principle 2: Brand Banks Govern the Hierarchy of Brands and Contact Points in Consumers' Minds

Brand banking is a proposition on how our minds manage the interplay between different brands and rank them according to preference. The following is a quick summary.

(1) A brand preference ladder exists in the minds of consumers for every relevant category, and which ranks brands on the rungs of this ladder.

(2) A brand bank exists in the minds of consumers for every brand they are familiar with.

(3) Master brand banks exist for "mother" brands, and they affect the brand banks that fall under them through the halo effect.

(4) A regular bank account exists for every contact point that a brand possesses.

(5) A brand bank account can be credited or debited not only by the brand's owners but also by other brands.

(6) A brand has to continually try to increase its bank balance.

(7) Inactivity leads to depreciation in the overall balance of the brand bank.

(8) A higher balance will result in a move up the preference ladder.

(9) The preference ladder is dynamic and is updated on every retrieval.

(10) Brands can avoid this constant struggle to stay ahead by achieving Wowability.

(11) A regular brand bank account becomes a premium account when contact points are turned into Wow points.

(12) Brands with premium accounts are always on the top rung of the preference ladder, followed by brands with the highest regular bank account balance.

Principle 3: Contact Points Are Key to a Brand's Future

Contacts points are all experiences through which consumers directly or indirectly come into contact with a brand, or obtain information about it. They can encompass any aspect of a brand, and are perceived and experienced differently by different consumers. Such dynamism adds to the difficulty in managing them.

Contact points are important because consumers derive value from them. The total value of a brand is the sum of all individual contact points. Because of the uniqueness in the way they combine and react with each other, the whole is usually greater than the sum of its parts.

Principle 4: A Consumer's Perception of a Brand's Value is Derived From the Sum of All the Individual Contact Points that She is Familiar With

In line with this principle, brands that want to increase their total value and move up the preference ladder have two ways to do so.

(A) Increase the number of contact points that the consumer is familiar with.
Generally, as the consumer becomes familiar with more of a brand's contact points, the value of the brand increases in his or her mind. Communicational contact points convey information about the various contact points and their value to consumers who may not be aware of them.

(B) Increase the value of contact points familiar to the consumer.
Identifying and improving strategic contact points can increase the total value of the brand. The tools discussed in Chapters 8 and 9 can pinpoint which contact points to focus on.

Principle 5: All Contact Points Can Be Categorized as Functional, Emotional, or Communicational

Functional contact points directly relate to a brand's functional aspects, such as features, quality, and effectiveness. For a lot of brands, technology is the main driver for the development of functional contact points. As brands acquire similar access to technology, it becomes harder to exceed expectations and sustain Wowability in these contact points.

Emotional contact points are less tangible but arguably more important. Brands should pay close attention to them as they are very difficult for competitors to replicate. Examples of emotional contact points include the brand story, brand leadership, and design.

Communicational contact points are often channels through which functional and emotional contact points are conveyed to consumers. They can have both functional and emotional value. Examples of communicational contact points include advertising, public relations, and word-of-mouth.

Principle 6: Wowability is Achieved When Companies Turn Contact Points Into Wow Points

Each contact point has an inherent value. A Wow point is created when the value provided by the contact point exceeds the value that consumers expect from it.

For example, consumers may have expectations about the kind of functions the average notebook should be able to perform. This forms the basis of their expectations for notebooks on the market. If a brand then introduces several new features that none of its competitors have, the brand turns features into its Wow point for as long as consumer expectations continue to be exceeded in this aspect. When other notebook brands replicate these features, the Wow point is eroded and downgraded to a contact point. Other Wow points could include design. The value of emotional Wow points is not as easily eroded because it is practically impossible to replicate the emotional connection that results from great design. Brands like Apple devote substantial resources to design, and it is not easy for a competing brand that does not have the same attitude or resources to achieve Wowability in this contact point. Functional contact points are relatively easier to copy and are more difficult to defend.

Principle 7: Choosing Key Contact Points and Developing A Strategy to Convert Them Into Wow Points Are Essential Steps Toward Achieving Wowability

Consumers attach varying importance and expectations to the different contact points of a brand. The same contact point may also be ranked more important in some product categories than others. It is crucial to identify the key contact points in your industry in order to know which ones to focus on.

Brands should not try to excel in all of their contact points for four main reasons. First, they are unlikely to have the resources to make significant improvements to every contact point. Second, consumers do not attach the same level of importance to all contact points. It is inefficient to target them all as consumers are unlikely to recognize the improvements made to the less important ones. Third, brands should position themselves strongly in the minds of consumers, and targeting select contact points is key to effective positioning.

Last, focusing on a specific set of contact points gets all the stakeholders of the company on the same page by creating a clear and definitive goal for them to work toward. This makes it more probable that the company will succeed.

But while reliance on a few Wow points may be key to Wowability, it is not without risks. These risks can be reduced by identifying the correct contact points to develop, and by defending them aggressively.

Principle 8: Once Wowability Has Been Achieved, It Needs to be Sustained by Managing Consumer Expectations

As expectations rise, and competitors ruthlessly copy Wow points, Wowability will become increasingly difficult to sustain. The following steps can then be taken:

(A) Create new Wow points. Improve total value by identifying potentially important contact points, and turning them into Wow points. Singapore Airlines is renowned for its service, but has sought to create more Wow points by improving other contact points, for instance, providing larger and more comfortable seats.

(B) Manage expectations. Brands can also sustain Wowability by managing consumer expectations through pricing and regulating release dates.

Price is an interesting contact point. It has both functional and emotional value, and can be a Wow point when it is low (providing value for money, a functional aspect) or when it is high (indicating a luxury buy, an emotional aspect). In general, however, the higher the price, the higher consumer expectations of the brand. This may seem to contradict the thinking that brands with Wowability can command higher prices. They can still do this, but it is important to be aware of price elasticity. Also keep in mind that higher prices raise the expectations of consumers and make it harder to sustain Wowability.

Release dates are applicable to brands that roll out new products on a regular basis. Scheduled releases mean that consumers won't be disappointed because you have not immediately released a new Wow version of your product. It also allows each version to go through its natural life cycle and increases the longevity of the brand's Wowability.

Principle 9: Create Barriers to Discourage Competition

Creating barriers is important for brands with Wowability. Sustaining a Wow point would be next to impossible if competitors were easily able to replicate your improvements in their own products. There can be different strategies for different contact points in this regard, yet one of the most common overall is through registration of the brand's intellectual properties.

Principle 10: Brands Must Always be on the Lookout for Opportunities to Create Disruptive Wow points

Ultimately, Wowability is destined to decline due to rising expectations. Although it is possible to manage expectations, it is inevitable that they will rise over time. Disruptive Wowability, which includes disruptive technologies and business models, redefines the competitive landscape. Embracing it means going beyond current expectations and forging new ones by which everyone else in the industry will be judged. Michael Dell's business model, which cut out the middleman, transformed the computer industry; consumers got their computers for much less than from competitors who were using traditional retail business models. When you redefine the competitive landscape, you are in fact rejuvenating your brand and creating a new Wow point for it.

The Way Ahead

The fate of every successful brand hinges on a few contact points to which it dedicates time and effort to fine tuning and improving. The Starbucks brand would be doomed if its coffee was seen as no different from a generic cup. However, that is hardly likely to happen soon. Its management will simply not allow the brand bank accounts of Starbucks to deteriorate to such an extent. It is a safe bet that the company will keep adding to its bank accounts. It is the same story for BMW. It is almost inconceivable that BMW would allow itself to lose its advantage in the performance and design contact points.

Companies with Wowability are aware that they are known for a few Wow points, and they defend those Wow points aggressively. Despite fully comprehending the risk that they take in relying on a few contact points, the reality is that successful brands do select a few Wow points to focus on, and they work hard to sustain them.

Expectations Are Everywhere

Everyone has expectations, and not just of brands. Expectations are how our brain converts relevant experiences into benchmarks for future ones. While not without their pitfalls, expectations provide us with a way to quickly assess new situations.

I have formed WCG—the Wowability Consulting Group—together with other similar-minded professionals who value exceeding expectations. WCG aims to provide guidance on implementing Wowability. Please contact me at wowability@gmail.com if you have any comments or further questions about this book, or if you would like to discuss implementing Wowability in your organization.

APPENDIX I:
Wowability Surveys

Objective

Between May and June 2006, my colleagues at ADK and I conducted two surveys to test selected brands for Wowability; and to discover the relationship between Wowability and factors like preference, emotional value, and functional value, among others. Both surveys were conducted online from Singapore.

Wow Score Survey

Details

The Wow Score survey is a tool that can be used by managers to learn more about their brand in relation to competitor brands. This is done by examining how each brand exceeds expectations in its various contact points and using this information to measure the Wowability of the brand as a whole.

Our survey focused on the MP3 player industry, specifically the Sony MP3 player, the Apple iPod, and the Creative ZEN series. Respondents had to be familiar with the MP3 player industry, particularly with the marketing campaigns of the three product lines. The 12 contact points we isolated were Performance, Features, Price, Design, Customer Service, Brand Story, Leadership, User Experience, Advertising, Sales Promotions, Recommendations (Word-of-Mouth), and Trade Shows.

Methodology

All together, 184 respondents participated in the online survey. Respondents were asked to rate the following on a Seven-point scale:

a. The importance of each contact point when considering an MP3 player purchase
b. How familiar they were with the contact points of each MP3 player
c. By how much, if at all, the brands had exceeded their expectations for the given contact points

From responses to the first question, the average importance, or Ideal Score was obtained. The Exceeded Expectations Score was then divided by the Ideal Score and multiplied by 100; the resulting Ideal or Wow Score tells managers by how much their brand has exceeded expectations in a contact point, relative to the Ideal Score.

Findings

Functional contact points (performance, features, and price) were rated as the most important contact points when considering an MP3 player purchase. Sales promotions were rated as the next most important, followed by design, user experience, and recommendations.

Sony MP3 had an average score of 4.28, compared to Apple iPod's 4.55, and Creative ZEN's 4.37. When the results were divided by the Ideal Score in this survey (5.33), Apple iPod came closest to exceeding consumer expectations.

Wowability Factors Survey

I have mentioned this survey, along with the Wow score survey, a few times throughout the book, especially in chapters 1, 3, 5, and 6. The correlation tables have been created using data from this survey.

Details

For this survey, 16 well-known brands from diverse industries were selected; some brands (but not all) were market leaders.

The brands were rated on a seven-point scale according to how well they did on eight factors: Delight, Preference, Reputation, Wow Factor, Functional Value, Emotional Value, Loyalty, and Exceeding Expectations.

Methodology

244 respondents participated in the online survey.

List of Brands

1. Singapore Airlines
2. Nokia
3. McDonald's
4. Google
5. Coca-Cola
6. Apple iPod
7. Starbucks
8. Creative
9. Toyota
10. Samsung
11. Lexus
12. Apple Mac
13. Apple
14. Dell
15. Ben & Jerry's
16. Lenovo

Findings

By plotting the trend lines, we were able to test the correlation between each of the eight factors and Exceeding Expectations. Delight (0.92) had the highest correlation with Exceeding Expectations, followed by Preference (0.90), Emotional Value (0.85) and Functional Value (0.78).

Appendix II:
The Wowability Framework

The Wowability framework allows us to identify those contact points that would be best to turn into Wow points. This process starts from a database of raw contact points, i.e., a general pool of contact points that the brand has or could have. To begin, raw contact points are collated from several sources:

(A) Market/customer surveys
(B) Company employees
(C) Consultants and other industry experts

This pool of contact points should be a mix of existing contact points and new or proposed contact points.

Figure 12.1: The segregation of the pool of contact points

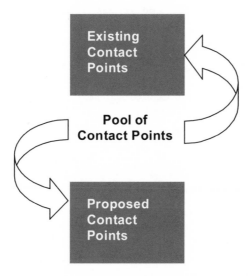

Let's take Nokia as an example to illustrate this concept. A pool of Nokia's contact points is derived from customer surveys, discussions with Nokia's management and employees, and from consultants and other industry experts.

Figure 12.2: Nokia's pool of contact points

Pool of Contact Points			
Mother Brand	User Friendliness	Weight of the Phone	Affordability
Size (Handset)	Camera	Music	Internet Connectivity
Color	Design	Durability	Accessories
S/W Applications	Resolution	Music Clarity	Reduced Weight

These contact points are then divided into existing and desirable new contact points.

Figure 12.3: Dividing Nokia's pool of contact points

Existing Contact Points			
Mother Brand	User Friendliness	Weight of the Phone	Affordability
Size (Handset)	Camera	Music	Internet Connectivity
Color	Design	Accessories	S/W Applications
Durability			

New Contact Points			
Resolution	Music Clarity	Reduced Weight	

At this stage, two approaches are used to identify viable contact points from the pool of existing contact points, and the pool of new contact points, respectively. Viable contact points are those that can be turned into Wow points.

The "Existing Contact Point" Approach

Figure 12.4: Illustration of the "Existing Contact Point" Matrix

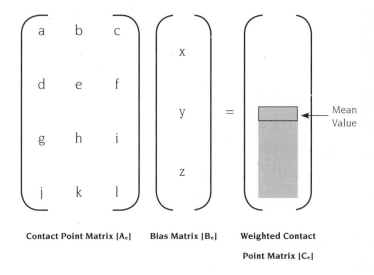

Contact Point Matrix $[A_e]$ Bias Matrix $[B_e]$ Weighted Contact Point Matrix $[C_e]$

A given number of contact points, n, is structured into an "n x 3" Matrix, **Matrix $[A_e]$**. A "3 x 1" Bias Matrix, **Matrix $[B_e]$**, is then formulated based on the weightage given to the consumer's (x), company's (y), and consultant's (z) point of view. For a consumer-oriented existing product, the consumer is given the highest weightage (total out of 10). For a new product, on the other hand, the company and consultant get the upper hand. The aggregate of the three weights is 10, assuming ratings on a scale of 1 to 10.

$[C_e] = [A_e] \times [B_e]$, is then calculated, where $[C_e]$ is the "n x 1" order matrix, which grades or ranks the contact points. This matrix lists the weighted contact points. Viable contact points are identified based on the mean of all the rankings.

The figures below show how the three matrices could look in the case of Nokia.

Figure 12.5: Nokia's Existing Contact Point Weighted Matrix

Contact Points	Customer	Company	Consultant	Multiply contact point matrix with bias matrix	Bias Matrix
Mother Brand	7.8	10	8		
User Friendliness	7.8	9	9		5
Weight of the Phone	6.4	7	7		
Affordability	7.9	7	8		
Size(Handset)	6.3	7	9		
Camera	5.9	7	6		
Music	6.6	6	6		3
Internet Connectivity	5	8	4		
Color	6.8	7	8		
Design	7.8	7	8		
Durability	9	10	9		2
Accessories	6.3	8	7		
S/W Applications	7.7	10	8		

The above ratings for each contact point would have been derived on a 10-point performance rating scale from surveys (customer), company insights (company management views) and opinions from consultants (consultant views). A score of 10 here means that the brand is doing well on this contact point.

The bias matrix shows the recommended bias for this category, where the top row is the weight given to the customer's opinion, and the second and third rows represent the weight given to the company's and the consultant's opinions, respectively. From the contact point matrix and the weighted contact point matrix, the resultant matrix can then be calculated. For example, the rating for the contact point of Durability can be calculated as such: $(9 \times 5) + (10 \times 3) + (9 \times 2) = 93$. Next, a mean of all the ratings should be calculated and the resulting figure treated as a cutoff point for selecting viable contact points. This eliminates all non viable contact points, or contact points that score below the mean (the shaded area). Consultants have the liberty of selecting one or two contact points from the top of the shaded area as viable contact points, since these contact points, although they didn't make the grade, may have high potential for future success.

Figure 12.6: Nokia's Existing Contact Points Resultant Matrix

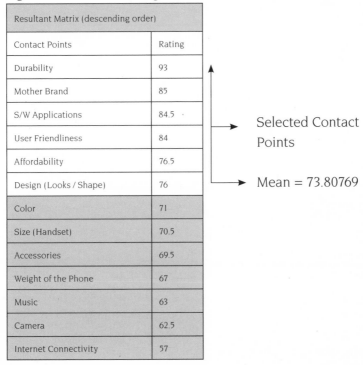

Resultant Matrix (descending order)	
Contact Points	Rating
Durability	93
Mother Brand	85
S/W Applications	84.5
User Friendliness	84
Affordability	76.5
Design (Looks / Shape)	76
Color	71
Size (Handset)	70.5
Accessories	69.5
Weight of the Phone	67
Music	63
Camera	62.5
Internet Connectivity	57

Selected Contact Points

Mean = 73.80769

The viable contact points (unshaded) obtained from the resultant matrix are now classified as emotional, communicational, and functional. Each contact point is rated on a scale of 1 to 10 for its strengths on all three: Emotional, Communicational, and Functional (ECF) parameters.

Figure 12.7: Nokia's Existing Contact Points Product Matrix [D_e]

Contact Points	Emotional	Communicational	Functional	Multiply contact points with rating	Rating
Durability	6	5	9		93
Mother Brand	8	9	4		85
S/W Applications	9	6	0		84.5
User Friendliness (GUI)	5	5	9		84
Affordability	3	8	8		76.5
Design (Looks/Shape)	8	6	0		76

A product matrix (Figure 12.8) is obtained by scalar multiplication of ECF with the ratings. These values denote the relative importance of key aspects of the selected existing contact points.

Figure 12.8: Nokia's Existing Contact Points Final Matrix

Contact Points	Emotional	Communicational	Functional	Mean
Durability	558	465	837	
Mother Brand	680	765	340	501.4444
S/W Applications	760.5	507	0	
User Friendliness	420	420	756	
Affordability	229.5	612	612	
Design (Looks/Shape)	608	456	0	

A second filter is applied by taking the mean again and considering the factors that lie above the threshold value. The ECF Parameters highlighted are those we need to focus on through marketing, advertising, and innovation in order to turn these contact points into Wow points.

The "New Contact Points" Approach

In the case of new contact points, we go through many of the same steps described earlier. However the bias matrix is more heavily weighted in favor of the consultant's point of view.

Figure 12.9: Nokia's New Contact Points and Bias Matrices

New Contact Points	Customer	Company	Consultant	Multiply with bias	Bias matrix
Resolution	7.8	7	8		2
Music Clarity	7.5	2	4		3
Reduced Weight	8.2	5	7		5

The above ratings for each contact point would have been derived on a 10-point importance scale from surveys, company insights, and opinions from consultants. The two matrices above are multiplied to obtain the weighted new contact points matrix.

Figure 12.10: Nokia's New Contact Points Resultant Matrix

New Resultant Matrix	
Contact Points	Rating
Resolution	76.6
Reduced Weight	41
Music Clarity	32.5

Selected
New Point

Mean =
50.03333

With this matrix, a mean score can be calculated to select viable contact points. In this case, the company could think of focusing on better screen resolution.

Figure 12.11: Nokia's New Contact Points Product Matrix

ECF Matrix

Contact Points	Emotional	Communicational	Functional	Multiply by Rating	Rating
Resolution	6	5	9		76.6

Contact Points	Emotional	Communicational	Functional	Mean
Resolution	459.6	383	689.4	510.667

As further analysis shows that this is primarily a functional contact point, the company will need to turn to innovation and R&D to convert this attribute into a Wow point.

ENDNOTES

CHAPTER 1

1 Jefferson, T. *Thomas Jefferson*: *Writings*: *Autobiography*. New York, 1984. Library of America.

2 Harris, B. Why a "Satisfied Customer" is Bad News for Your Brand, and Your Business. 24-7, 2006. http://www.24-7pressrelease.com/ view_press_release.php?rID=13463& tf7sid=bb6203836bdaf392bc510abfe5c2cba0

3 Aufreiter, N.A., Elzinga, D., Gordon J.W. Better Branding. *The McKinsey Quarterly*, 4. Abstract. McKinsey, 2003. http://www.mckinseyquarterly. com/Better_branding_1349_abstract

4 Rusch, R.D. Muji: Commonly Unique. Brandchannel, 2001. http://www.brandchannel.com/features_profile.asp?pr_id=14

5 Gogoi, P. The Serious Cachet of "Secret Brands." *BusinessWeek*, 2005. http://www.igorinternational.com/press/business-wk6-branding-secret-brands.php

6 Cohen, B. The Wow Effect: How One Restaurateur Continues to Delight Customers. *Cornell Hotel and Restaurant Administration Quarterly*. 1997. Volume 38, Issue 2, Pgs 74-75.

7 Ibid.

8 Ibid.

9 Cohen, B. *W.O.W. 2000*. Atlanta, Georgia: Savannah Corporation, 1997.

10 Tiscali Film & TV. Steven Spielberg Filmography. Tuscali, 2007. http://www.tiscali.co.uk/entertainment/film/biographies/steven_spielberg_films/2

11 Graydon, D. E.T. The Extra Terrestrial (1982). BBC, 2002. http://www.bbc.co.uk/films/2002/03/19/et_the_extra_terrestrial_2002_review.shtml

CHAPTER 2

1 Hof, R. Jeff Bezos on Word-of-Mouth Power. *BusinessWeek*, 2004. http://www.businessweek.com/magazine/content/04_31/b3894101.htm

2 Rucinski, T. TV Output with the Samsung SGH=D600. iMobile, 2006. http://www.imobile.com.au/PhoneReviews/default. asp?ID=reviewsjan0601

3 Ewing, J. Nokia Gets Design Conscious–Again. *BusinessWeek*, 2006. http://www.businessweek.com/globalbiz/content/nov2006/gb20061129_673395.htm?chan=globalbiz_europe_today's+top+story

4 Singer, L. Supersize Me Interview. BBC, 2004. http://www.bbc.co.uk/dna/collective/A2987175

5 Zhang, S., Kardes, F.R., Cronley, M.L. Comparative Advertising: Effects of Structural Alignability on Target Brand Evaluations. *Journal of Consumer Psychology.* 2002. Volume 12, No 4, Pgs 303-11.

6 Guyon, J. The Magic Touch LVMH Chief Bernard Arnault Runs Dozens of Luxury Brands, From Moet & Chandon to Thomas Pink. But Just One of Them—Louis Vuitton—Brings in 60% of the Conglomerate's Profits. *Fortune Magazine,* 2004.
http://money.cnn.com/magazines/fortune/fortune_archive/2004/09/06/380345/index.htm

7 Macworld staff. Apple iPod Silhouette Campaign Scoops Gold Awards. *Macworld,* 2005 http://www.macworld.co.uk/news/index.cfm?RSS&NewsID=12790

8 Interbrand staff. (2007). The Best Global Brands 2006 Report. Interbrand, 2007. http://www.interbrand.com/best_brands_2007.asp

9 International Olympic Committee staff. IOC and Samsung Extend Partnership to 2016. International Olympic Committee, 2007.
http://www.olympic.org/uk/organisation/commissions/marketing/full_story_uk.asp?id=2134

10 Samsung staff (2005, April 25). Samsung Press Center, 2005. Retrieved January 12, 2008
http://www.samsung.com/ph/presscenter/samsunginthephilippines/sponsoredevents_20050425_0000117656.asp

11 Suwon Samsung Bluewings staff. History of Bluewings. Samsung Bluewings, 2007
http://www.fcbluewings.com/eng/history/history1.asp

12 CPO staff. Samsung Electronics Reports Fourth Quarter Financial Results. Cell Phone Observer, 2007
http://www.cellphoneobserver.com/_samsung_electronics_reports_fourth_quarter_financial_results_jan_12

13 Berner, R., Kiley, D. Global Brands. *BusinessWeek,* 2005.
http://www.businessweek.com/magazine/content/05_31/b3945098.htm

14 Rocks, D., Moon, I. Samsung Design. *BusinessWeek,* 2004.
http://www.businessweek.com/magazine/content/04_48/b3910003.htm

15 Ibid.

16 Ibid.

17 Samsung staff. Quality Education & Training. Samsung, 2007.
http://www.samsung.com/global/business/semiconductor/support/qualitymanagement/support_QualityEducationTraining.html

18 Samsung staff. Samsung Hall of Awards. Samsung, 2007.
http://www.samsung.com/my/products/awards/sme_hall_of_awards.html

19 Moon, I. Camp Samsung. *BusinessWeek*, 2006.
    http://www.businessweek.com/magazine/content/06_27/b3991052.htm
20 Interbrand staff. The Best Global Brands 2006 Report. Interbrand, 2007.
    http://www.interbrand.com/best_brands_2007.asp

CHAPTER 3

1 Da Vinci, L. Quoted in his personal compilation of *The Notebooks*. 1509–
   1518
2 Harley-Davidson staff. H.O.G Fly & Ride. Harley-Davidson.
   http://www.harley-davidson.com/wcm/Content/Pages/HOG/fly_and_
   ride.jsp?locale=en_us
3 Toyota staff. History of Toyota. Toyota. http://www.toyota.co.jp/en/
   history/1950.html
4 Taylor, A. The Birth of the Prius. *Fortune Magazine*, 2006. Volume 153.
   Issue 4, Pgs 24-27.
5 Toyota staff. Vision and Philosophy. Toyota. http://www.toyota.co.jp/en/
   vision/traditions/jan_feb_03.html
6 Toyota staff. Overview: New Toyota Hybrid Cars Information. Toyota,
   2007.
   http://www.toyota-camry.com/overview.php
7 Taylor, A. The Americanization of Toyota. *Fortune Magazine*, 2003. Volume
   148. Issue 12, Pgs 54-58
8 AP staff. Toyota Aims to Break GM Global Sales Record in 2009. USA
   Today, 2007.
   http://www.usatoday.com/money/autos/2007-08-31-toyota-sales_N.htm
9 Taylor, A. The birth of the Prius. *Fortune Magazine*, 2006. Volume 153.
   Issue 4, Pgs 24 – 27.
10 Interbrand staff. *The Best Global Brands* 2006 *Report*. Interbrand, 2007.
    http://www.interbrand.com/best_brands_2007.asp
11 Ewing, J. Nokia Gets Design Conscious–Again. *BusinessWeek*, 2006.
    http://www.businessweek.com/globalbiz/content/nov2006/gb20061129_
    673395.htm?chan=globalbiz_europe_today's+top+story
12 Van Hout, M. Getting Emotional with Tamer Nakisci. Design &
    Emption, 2005. http://www.design-emotion.com/2005/12/12/getting-
    emotional-with-tamer-nakisci
13 Nokia staff. Nokia Design. Nokia, 2003.
    http://www.nokia.com/NOKIA_COM_1/About_Nokia/Sidebar_Teasers/
    Backgrounders/nokiadesignbackgrounder.pdf
14 Ibid.

15 Lewis, P. The Perpetual Crisis Machine. *Fortune Magazine*, 2005.,
    Retrieved from CNN Money.
    http://money.cnn.com/magazines/fortune/fortune_archive/2005/09/19/
    8272909/index.htm

16 Ibid.

17 Ibid.

18 Walkowich, R. Macs at Work? Night Fire and a PowerBook. MacIntosh
    Articles, 1996.
    http://www.mymac.com/showarticle.php?id=1403

19 Evans, B. and Hoffman, T. Apple Makes Mac OS X the Default Operating
    System on All Macs. Apple Press Release, Macworld Expo San
    Francisco, 2002.
    http://www.apple.com/pr/library/2002/jan/07macosx.html

20 Van Buskirk, E. Perspective: The Secret of iPod's Scroll Wheel. CNET
    News, 2004.
    http://news.com.com/2010-1041_3-5375101.html

21 Marsal , K. iPod: How Big Can It Get? Apple Insider, 2006.
    http://www.appleinsider.com/articles/06/05/24/ipod_how_big_can_it_
    get.html

22 Ibid.

23 Morningstar staff. Morningstar Quicktake Report: S&P 500 Index
    Data. Morningstar, 2006. http://quicktake.morningstar.com/stocknet/
    Snapshot.aspx?Country=USA&Symbol=AAPL&pmts=SS2

24 Ibid.

25 Zborowski, K. Yoneyama, V. and Mulhern, J. Computing news: Apple's
    iPod. University of Pennsylvania, Office of Information Systems and
    Computing, 2003.
    http://www.upenn.edu/computing/home/news/2001/ipod.html

26 Kerris, N. and Dowling, S. Apple reinvents the phone with iPhone.
    Apple Press Release, 2007.
    http://www.apple.com/pr/library/2007/01/09iphone.html

27 Apple staff. Apple iPhone. Apple, 2007. http://www.apple.com/iphone/
    easysetup/getready.html

CHAPTER 4

1 Eisner, Michael. *Be Our Guest: Perfecting the Art of Customer Service*. New
   York: Disney Press, 2003.

2 Beneli, Iris. Selective Attention and Arousal. University, Northridge,
   1997. http://www.csun.edu/~vcpsy00h/students/arousal.htm

3 Wal-Mart Stores staff. Corporate Facts: Wal-Mart by the Numbers. Wal-
   Mart. http://www.walmartfacts.com/FactSheets/3142007_Corporate_
   Facts.pdf

4   Fried, Ina. Apple Spends a Bundle on iPod Ads. CNET News, 2005. http://news.com.com/Apple+spends+a+bundle+on+iPod+ads/2100-1047_3-5978598.html

5   Build-A-Bear Workshop staff. Build-A-Bear Workshop: International Locations. Build-A-Bear Workshop, 2007. http://www.buildabear.com/aboutUs/contactUs/FindAStore/#international

6   *BusinessWeek* staff. Hot Growth Special Report 2006. *BusinessWeek*, 2006. http://www.businessweek.com/hot_growth/2006/company/40.htm

7   Plowright, T. (2007). Build-A-Bear. About.com: Travel with Kids, 2007. http://travelwithkids.about.com/od/familyfunplaces/p/buildabear.htm

8   Ibid.

9   Starbucks Coffee Company staff. A Brief History of Starbucks. Starbucks U.K., 2005. http://starbucks.co.uk/en-GB/_About+Starbucks/History+of+Starbucks.htm

10 Starbucks Coffee Company staff. About Us: Starbucks Mission Statement. Starbucks, 2007. http://www.starbucks.com/aboutus/environment.asp

11 Thompson, A. A., and Strickland, J.A. Starbucks Case Study. Strategic Management: Concepts and Cases. The McGraw-Hill Companies, 1997. http://www.mhhe.com/business/management/thompson/11e/case/starbucks-2.html

12 Stein, N. Crisis in a Coffee Cup. CNNMoney.com, 2002. http://money.cnn.com/magazines/fortune/fortune_archive/2002/12/09/333463/

13 Schultz , H. *Pour Your Heart Into It: How Starbucks Built a Company One Cup at a Time.* New York, NY: Hyperion, 1999.

14 Thuan, T. Starbucks Corporation. 2003. http://mywebpages.comcast.net/ThuanTran/business/starbucks.pdf

15 Thompson, A. A., and Strickland, J.A. Starbucks Case Study. Strategic Management: Concepts and Cases. The McGraw-Hill Companies, 1997. http://www.mhhe.com/business/management/thompson/11e/case/starbucks-2.html

16 Ibid.

17 Kirbyson, G. Howard Schultz-Uncommon Grounds. Brandchannel, 2004. http://www.brandchannel.com/print_page.asp?arid=47&section=career

18 Bonamici, K., and Serwer, A. Hot Starbucks To Go. *Fortune Magazine*, 2004. Volume 149. Issue 1, Pgs 58-65. Retrieved from Business Source Premier database.

19 Kirbyson, G. Howard Schultz-Uncommon Grounds. Brandchannel, 2004. http://www.brandchannel.com/print_page.asp?ar_id=47&section=career

20 Weber, G. Preserving the Starbucks Counter Culture. Workforce Management, 2005. http://www.workforce.com/section/06/feature/23/94/44/index.html

21 Barnett, A. A. Perks for Part Timers-Starbucks Corp. BNET.com:
    Business and Health, 1996.
    http://findarticles.com/p/articles/mi_m0903/is_n9_v14/ai_18687795
22 Ibid.
23 Smith, S. S. Grounds for Success: Interview with Starbucks CEO Howard
    Schultz. *Entrepreneur Magazine*, 1998. http://www.entrepreneur.com/
    magazine/entrepreneur/1998/may/15582.html
24 Ibid.
25 Holmes, S. Starbucks: Keeping the Brew Hot. *BusinessWeek*, 2001.
    http://www.businessweek.com/magazine/content/01_32/b3744014.htm
26 Ibid.
27 Helm, B. and Goudreau, J. Is Starbucks pushing prices too high?
    BusinessWeek, 2007.
    http://www.businessweek.com/bwdaily/dnflash/content/jul2007/
    db20070801_030871.htm
28 Starbucks Coffee Company staff. A Brief History of Starbucks.
    Starbucks U.K., 2005. http://starbucks.co.uk/en-GB/_About+Starbucks/
    History+of+Starbucks.htm

CHAPTER 5

1 Grove, A. S. *Only the Paranoid Survive: How to Exploit the Crisis Points that
   Challenge Every Company*. New York: Currency Doubleday, 1999.
2 BMW Manufacturing staff. Education and Research: BMW ITRC. BMW
   Manufacturing Co. http://www.bmwusfactory.com/education/bmw_itrc/
3 Florian, J. BMW's New Windshield Display. AME Info/Emap
   Communications, 2007. http://www.ameinfo.com/132338.html
4 *The Sydney Morning Herald*. The Gadget that Changed the World. AP, 2007.
   http://www.smh.com.au/news/phones--pdas/the-gadget-that-changed-
   the-world/2007/05/18/1178995417710.html
5 Nokia Multimedia Communications. Nokia and Carl Zeiss Join Forces to
   Offer Enhanced Imaging for Camera Phone Users. Nokia, 2005. http://
   press.nokia.com/PR/200504/991483_5.html
6 Praxiom Research Group Limited staff. ISO 9000: An Introduction.
   Praxiom Research Group, 2006. http://www.praxiom.com/iso-intro.htm
7 Deuter USA Inc. Staff. Company: Deuter Timeline. Deuter U.S.
   http://www.deuterusa.com/company/time.php
8 Pro Mountain Sports staff. Packs - Deuter Materials. Pro Mountain
   Sports. http://www.promountainsports.com/packs.shtml?
   http://www.promountainsports.com/packs-deuter-materials.shtml
9 Backcountry.com staff. Deuter Kid Comfort I. Backcountry.com
   http://www.backcountry.com/store/DTR0001/c100000008/s100000044/
   Deuter-Kid-Comfort-I.html

10 Liebeskind, D. (2004). What Makes Rolex Tick? *Stern Business*. Retrieved July 8, 2006, from New York University, Leonard N. Stern School of Business website: http://www.stern.nyu.edu/Sternbusiness/fall_winter_2004/rolex.html

11 Hall, G. Why Every Man Should Own a High Quality Fine Watch. EzineArticles.com, 2007. http://ezinearticles.com/?Why-Every-Man-Should-Own-A-High-Quality-Fine-Watch&id=294674

12 Motorola staff. About Motorola University: The Inventors of Six Sigma. Motorola, 2007. http://www.motorola.com/content.jsp?globalObjectId=3079

13 Forini, J. Quality Over Price, Or Price Over Quality—Six Sigma. EzineArticles.com, 2007. http://ezinearticles.com/?Quality-Over-Price,-Or-Price-Over-Quality-Six-Sigma&id=606079

14 Bonamici, K. King Gillette Decides to Throw Away the Blades. *Fortune Magazine*, 2005. Volume 151. Issue 11, Pg 38.

15 Liu, S. S. and Johnson, K. F. The Automatic Country of Origin Effects on Brand Judgments. *Journal of Advertising*. 2005. Volume 34. Pgs 87-97

16 Haagen-Dazs staff. Company History: The Idea for Haagen-Dazs Dates Back to Early 1920s. Haagen-Dazs. http://www.haagen-dazs.com/company/history.aspx

17 Krebs, M. (2006, May 23). A Short History of Japanese Luxury Cars. *BusinessWeek*, 2006. http://www.businessweek.com/autos/content/may2006/bw20060523_579325.htm?chan=search

18 Chandler, C. Full Speed Ahead. *Fortune Magazine*, 2005. http://money.cnn.com/magazines/fortune/fortune_archive/2005/02/07/8250430/index.htm

19 ICFAI: Centre for Management Research. (2003). Toyota's Kaizen Experience. Retrieved July 11, 2006, from ICFAI website: http://icmr.icfai.org/casestudies/catalogue/Operations/OPER007.htm

20 Eisert, S. Applying Lean Toyota Production System Methods to Improving Health Care Systems. Paper presented at the annual meeting of the Economics of Population Health: Inaugural Conference of the American Society of Health Economists, TBA, Madison, WI, USA, October 05, 2006. http://www.allacademic.com/meta/p91599_index.html

21 Dawson, C. *Lexus: The Relentless Pursuit*. New Jersey: John Wiley & Sons, 2004.

22 Interbrand staff. *The Best Global Brands 2006 Report*. Interbrand, 2007. http://www.interbrand.com/best_brands_2007.asp

23 Taylor, A. The Birth of the Prius. *Fortune Magazine*, 2006. http://money.
cnn.com/magazines/fortune/fortune_archive/2006/03/06/8370702/
index.htm

24 Edmunds Inc. staff. Toyota Thinks Big: Full-Size Diesel and Hybrid
Coming to States in '09. Edmunds Inside Line, 2006. http://www.
edmunds.com/insideline/do/News/articleId=108724

25 Google staff. Google Milestones. Google Inc. http://www.google.com/
corporate/history.html

26 Yahoo! Finance staff. Google Inc. (GOOG). Yahoo! Finance, retrieved
September 13, 2007. http://finance.yahoo.com/q?s=GOOG

27 Knowledge@Wharton staff. A Search for Google's Success Turns Up
Two Words: Trust and Technology. Knowledge@Wharton, 2001. http://
knowledge.wharton.upenn.edu/article.cfm?articleid=435

28 Google staff. Technology Overview. Google. http://www.google.com/
corporate/tech.html

29 Google staff. Google, 2006 Annual Report. U.S. Securities and
Exchange Commission, retrieved April 23, 2007. http://www.sec.gov/
Archives/edgar/data/1288776/000119312507044494/d10k.htm

30 Google staff. Google AdWords. Google. http://adwords.google.com/
support/bin/answer.py?hl=en&answer=10949

31 Krol, C. Search Engine Marketing up 44% in 2005. B to B. Business
Source Premier database, 2006.Volume 91. Issue 1, Pgs 3-3

32 Vogelstein, F. and Burke, D. Google @ $165. *Fortune Magazine*. Business
Source Premier database, 2004. Volume 150. Issue 12, Pgs 98-110.

33 Wenzel, E. Web 2.0 Applications: Google vs. Yahoo vs. Microsoft vs.
The World. CNET.com, 2006.
http://reviews.cnet.com/4520-9239_7-6526615-1.html

CHAPTER 6

1 The Brand Council. *The Brand Council*. 2006. http://www.thebrandcouncil.
org/68548

2 Gross, M. Notes on Fashion. *The New York Times*, 1987. http://query.
nytimes.com/gst/fullpage.html?res=9B0DEFDB1439F930A35750C0A961
948260

3 Hays, C. L. Variable-Price Coke Machine Being Tested. *The New York
Times*, 1999. http://query.nytimes.com/gst/fullpage.html?res=9804E7D91
038F93BA15753C1A96F958260&sec=&spon=&pagewanted=1

4 Stew Leonard's staff. Company Story. Stew Leonard's.
http://www.stewleonards.com/html/about.cfm

5 Dawson, C. *Lexus: The Relentless Pursuit*. New Jersey: John Wiley & Sons,
2004

6 Spector, R., McCarthy, P. *The Nordstrom Way: The Inside Story of America's #1 Customer Service Company*. New York: John Wiley & Sons, 1996.

7 Wright, A. C. and Leckenby. Connections to Advertising. 2003. http://www.ciadvertising.org/sa/spring_03/382j/aclaire/Advertising.html

8 Ben & Jerry's staff. Flavor Locater. Ben & Jerry's. http://www.benjerry.com/our_products/flavor_locator/

9 Ben & Jerry's staff. American Pie. Ben & Jerry's. http://www.benjerry.com/americanpie

10 adidas staff. About adidas—The adidas Group at a Glance. adidas, 2007. http://www.press.adidas.com/en/DesktopDefault.aspx/tabid-28/41_read-113/

11 Miller, E. G., Kahn, B. E. Shades of Meaning: The Effect of Color and Flavor Names on Consumer Choice. *Journal of Consumer Research*. 2005. Volume 32. Issue 1, Pgs 86–92.

12 Timeline Index staff. Dell History. Timeline Index. http://www.timelineindex.com/content/view/1166

13 Dell staff. Dell at a Glance—Dell History. Dell, 2007. http://www.dell.com/content/topics/global.aspx/corp/background/en/facts?c=us&l=en&s=corp&~section=004

14 adidas staff. Advertising Campaign 2002. adidas, 2007. http://www.press.adidas.com/desktopdefault.aspx/tabid-131/

15 Forbes.com staff. Richard Branson. *Forbes*, 2007. http://www.forbes.com/lists/2006/10/2Y7I.html

16 Mihailescu, V. Disney Completes Pixar Acquisition. Softpedia, 2006. http://news.softpedia.com/news/Disney-Completes-Pixar-Acquisition-22980.shtml

17 Gallo, C. How to Wow 'Em Like Steve Jobs. *BusinessWeek*, 2006. http://www.businessweek.com/smallbiz/content/apr2006/sb20060406_865110.htm

18 Burrows, P. Apple's Cancer Scare. *BusinessWeek*, 2004. http://www.businessweek.com/technology/content/aug2004/tc2004082_9514_tc024.htm

19 Keefe, B. Market Wants to Know Apple Will Stay Fresh After Jobs. *The Sydney Morning Herald*, 2006.
http://www.smh.com.au/news/technology/market-wants-to-know-apple-will-stay-fresh-after-jobs/2006/03/24/1143083984252.html?page=2

20 Milligan, J. Hail and Farewell. *Bank Director Magazine* Archives-3rd Quarter 2006.
http://www.bankdirector.com/issues/articles.pl?article_id=11806

21 Russ, C. A Maxi History of the Original Mini. The Auto Channel, 2002. http://www.theautochannel.com/news/2002/09/26/148062.html

22 Volkswagen staff. Media Room: The Volkswagen Beetle—Success Story. Volkswagen, 2003. http://www.vw.com/newbeetle/brochures_download_pdf.html

23 Menzies, D. Painful Sport of Punch Buggy Still a Hit. CanWest Interactive, 2007. http://autos.canada.com/news/story.html?id=862fc865-d3b1-49c8-88a9-b73b7b90247a

24 Yahoo! Finance staff. Even as Mobile Phone Prices Plummet, Market Leader Nokia Dialed into Growth. Yahoo! Finance, 2007. http://biz.yahoo.com/ibd/071018/general.html?.v=1

25 Interbrand. Best Global Brands 2006. Interbrand, 2006. http://www.interbrand.com/best_brands_2006.asp

26 Yahoo! Finance staff. Even as Mobile Phone Prices Plummet, Market Leader Nokia Dialed into Growth. Yahoo! Finance, 2007, http://biz.yahoo.com/ibd/071018/general.html?.v=1

27 Steinbock, D. *The Nokia Revolution: The Story of an Extraordinary Company that Transformed an Industry*. New York: American Management Association, 2001.

28 Red Dot Design Award staff. Red Dot: Design Team of the Year 2003. Red Dot Design Award, 2003. http://en.red-dot.org/195.html

29 Steinbock, D. (2001, May 31).The Nokia Revolution: The Story of an Extraordinary Company that Transformed an Industry. New York: American Management Association.

30 Jurrien, I. Nokia Mobile Phone Design Studio. LetsGoMobile, 2007. http://www.letsgomobile.org/en/1695/nokia-design-studio/

31 Nokia staff. Press Releases: Art Meets State-of-the-Art: Exquisite Materials, Distinctive Details Unite to Create a Mobile Icon—the Nokia 8801. Nokia, 2005. http://www.nokia-asia.com/A4418023?newsid=988206

32 Nokia staff. Press Releases: Nokia Unifies and Strengthens Its Company-Wide Design Organization. Nokia, 2006. http://press.nokia.com/PR/200603/1037352_5.html

33 Ewing, J. and Moon, I. (2006, July 17). Staying Cool at Nokia. *BusinessWeek*, 2006. http://www.businessweek.com/magazine/content/06_29/b3993070.htm

34 Howard, T. Advertising & Marketing: A Nice-Smelling Man is Good to Find. USA *Today*, 2005. http://www.usatoday.com/money/advertising/adtrack/2005-07-17-axe-track_x.htm

35 AKQA staff. Clickmore. AKQA.com. http://awards.akqa.com/awards2006/axe/click/campaign.html

36 vikkvikk. Video: *axe-lynx-effect-spray-more-get-more vikk*. YouTube.com, 2007. http://www.youtube.com/watch?v=x8Im81EZ9Bg

CHAPTER 7

1 Alt, B. Interview: Flint McGlaughlin, Part II. EmailUniverse.com, 2001. http://emailuniverse.com/ezine-tips/?Interview:-Flint-McGlaughlin,-Part-II&id=297

2 Ray, M. L. A Decision Sequence Analysis of Developments in Marketing Communication. *Journal of Marketing*. 1973. Vol. 37. No.l, Pgs 29-38.

3 Heath, C. and Heath, D. The Curse of Knowledge. *Harvard Business Review*, 2007.

4 Ibid.

5 BBC News staff. Whassup? Boys Strike TV Deal. BBC News, 2000. http://news.bbc.co.uk/1/hi/entertainment/1023235.stm

6 Raugust, K. Bud-Weis-Er: Computer-Generated Frogs and Lizards Give Bud a Boost. *Animation World Magazine*, 1998. Issue 2.7. http://www.awn.com/mag/issue3.7/3.7pages/3.7raugustbud.html

7 Young, S. Getting More from Print Advertising. Perception Research Services International. http://www.prsresearch.com/Articles/getting%20more%20from%20print%20advertising.doc

8 Johnny Walker Advertisement. Fortune Magazine, 2005. Volume 152. Issue 10, Pgs 33–36.

9 Goldman, L., Burke, M. and Blakeley, K. Top 100 Celebrities. Forbes.com, 2006. http://www.forbes.com/lists/2006/53/RJGP.html

10 Schlecht, C. Celebrity's Impact on Branding. Columbia Business School, Centre on Global Brand Leadership, 2003. http://www.globalbrands.org/research/working/Celebrity_Branding.pdf

11 Accenture staff. Print Advertising. Accenture, 2007. http://www.accenture.com/Global/About_Accenture/Company_Overview/Advertising/Print_Advertising.htm

12 Lenovo staff. News: Ronaldinho Named a Lenovo Worldwide Brand Ambassador. Lenovo U.S., 2006. http://www.lenovo.com/news/us/en/2006/04/ronaldinho.html

13 Napit staff. FIFA World Player of the Year Award. Napit.co.uk, 2007. http://www.napit.co.uk/viewus/infobank/football/awards/worldplayer.php

14 Lenovo staff. As Newest Worldwide Sponsor of The Olympic Games, Lenovo Begins 150-Day Countdown to Torino. Lenovo Canada, 2005. http://www.lenovo.com/news/ca/en/2005/09/091305wwsponsor.html

15 Pourhadi, D. Apple Genius Says: Moo'ing Normal. The Unofficial Apple Weblog, 2006. http://www.tuaw.com/2006/06/21/apple-says-mooing-normal/

16 Carl, W. J. To Tell or Not to Tell? Word of Mouth Marketing Association, 2006. http://www.womma.org/wombat/presentations/womma_wombat_carl.pdf

17 FineWaters Media staff. Water & Celebrities. FineWaters Media, 2006. http://www.finewaters.com/Bottled_Water_News/Waters_Celebrities/Fiji_Water_Making_a_Scene.asp

18 Brennan, I. and Babin, A. L. Brand Placement Recognition: The Influence of Presentation Mode and Brand Familiarity. *Journal of Promotion Management*. 2004. Volume 10. Issue 1/2, Pgs 185-202.

19 Petrecca, L. Five-Second Ads Try to Counter TiVo. USA *Today*, 2006. http://www.usatoday.com/money/advertising/2006-07-05-5-second-ads-usat_x.htm

20 Vranica, S. Ad Buyers Eye Clear Channel's 'Blink' Spots. *The Wall Street Journal*, 2006. http://online.wsj.com/public/article/SB115975041919379557-LyKXy8oLn1sZbVS1e8WcDGv_i7U_20061009.html?mod=blogs

21 Lindgaard, G., Fernandes, G., Dudek, C. and Brown, J. Attention Web Designers: You Have 50 Milliseconds to Make a Good First Impression. *Behavior & Information Technology*. 2006. Volume 25. Number 2, Pgs 110-115.

22 Veloutsou, C. and O'Donnell, C. Exploring the Effectiveness of Taxis as an Advertising Medium. *International Journal of Advertising*. 2005. Volume 24. Issue 2, Pgs 217-240.

23 Kiley, D. Why Carl's Jr. and Paris Hilton are Doing It Right. *BusinessWeek*, 2005. http://www.businessweek.com/the_thread/brandnewday/archives/2005/06/why_carls_jr_an.html?chan=search

24 Gupta, S. Paris Hilton Ad Boosts Carl's Jr. Traffic. Media Post Publications, 2005. http://publications.mediapost.com/index.cfm?fuseaction=Articles.showArticleHomePage&art_aid=30627

25 Interbrand. *Best Global Brands* 2006. Interbrand, 2006. http://www.interbrand.com/best_brands_2006.asp

26 The Coca-Cola Company staff. The Chronicle of Coca-Cola. The Coca-Cola Company, 2007. http://www.thecoca-colacompany.com/heritage/chronicle_birth_refreshing_idea.html

27 Solar Navigator staff. Coca Cola History. Solar Navigator, 2007. http://www.solarnavigator.net/sponsorship/coca_cola.htm

28 Witzel, M. K. and Young-Witzel, G. *The Sparkling Story of Coca-Cola: An Entertaining History Including Collectibles, Coke Lore, and Calendar Girls*. Minnesota: Voyageur Press, 2006.

29 Grant, T. Royal Crown Company Inc. *International Directory of Company Histories*. St. James Press, 1998. Vol.23.

30 Ibid.

31 Regensbrg, A. SRCA Advertising Exhibit. Quipu. State Record Center and Archives, New Mexico Commission of Public Records, 2004. http://www.nmcpr.state.nm.us/pubs/quipu/quipu_apr04.pdf

32 Solar Navigator staff. Coca-Cola Advertising Slogans. Solar Navigator, 2007. http://www.solarnavigator.net/sponsorship/coca_cola_slogans.htm

33 Cartersville-Bartow County Convention and Visitors Bureau staff. World's First Coca-Cola Outdoor Wall Advertisement. Cartersville-Bartow County Convention and Visitors Bureau. http://www.notatlanta.org/firstsign.html

CHAPTER 8

1 Twain, M. *Mark Twain's Notebooks and Journals, Volume* III. California: University of California Press, 1883-1891.

CHAPTER 9

1 Mulcahy, S. Bomb-Proof Branding. Media Post Publications, 2005. http://publications.mediapost.com/index.cfm?fuseaction=Articles.showArticle&art_aid=36268

2 Reynolds, T. J. and Gutman, J. Laddering Theory, Method, Analysis, and Interpretation. Journal of *Advertising Research.* 1998. February/March. Pgs 79–99.

3 Duckett, R. H. Nurturing Creativity. First Tennessee Bank National Association, 2007. http://www.firsttennessee.com/index.cfm?Fuseaction=ExecutiveHighlightsNewsletter.ViewContent&Item=NuturingCreativity

4 Osborn, A. F. *Applied Imagination; Principles and Procedures of Creative Thinking.* South Carolina: Scribner Publishing House, 1957.

5 Osborn, A. F. *Your Creative Power.* Indiana: Purdue University Press, 1999.

6 Sutton, R. Eight Tips for Better Brainstorming. *BusinessWeek,* 2006. http://www.businessweek.com/innovate/content/jul2006/id20060726_517774.htm?chan=innovation_innovation+%2B+design_insight

7 *BusinessWeek* staff. Big Blue Brainstorm. *BusinessWeek,* 2006. http://www.businessweek.com/magazine/content/06_32/b3996062.htm?chan=tc&campaign_id=rss_tech

8 IBM staff. Press Releases: IBM Invests $100 Million in Collaborative Innovation Ideas. IBM, 2006. http://www-03.ibm.com/press/us/en/pressrelease/20605.wss

9 Big Blue Brainstorm. Op. cit.

10 IBM Invests $100 Million in Collaborative Innovation Ideas. Op. cit.

11 Buzan, B. and Buzan, T. *The Mind Map Book: Radiant Thinking-Major Evolution in Human Thought (3rd ed.)* London: BBC (BBC Active), 2003.

12 3M staff. McKnight Principles. 3M, 2007. http://solutions.3m.com/
wps/portal/3M/en_US/our/company/information/history/McKnight-
principles/

13 3M staff. Who We Are. 3M, 2007. http://solutions.3m.com/wps/portal/
3M/en_US/our/company/information/about-us/

14 Arndt, M. 3M's Seven Pillars of Innovation. *BusinessWeek*, 2006. http://
www.businessweek.com/innovate/content/may2006/id20060510_
682823.htm?chan=search

15 Ibid.

16 Lashinsky, A. Razr's Edge. Fortune Magazine, 2006. Retrieved from:
CNN Money. http://money.cnn.com/2006/05/31/magazines/fortune/
razr_greatteams_fortune/index.htm

17 Winnick, M. 5 Secrets to a Successful Launch. *Business* 2.0, 2006.
Volume 7, Issue 8, Pgs 93-100. Retrieved from Business Source Premier
database.

18 Salter, C. Moto's Mojo. *Fast Company Magazine*, 2006. Issue 104.
http://www.fastcompany.com/magazine/104/moto.html

19 Wasserman, T. Moto: Razor Sharp Again. *Brandweek*, 2005. Volume 46,
Issue 36, Pgs 36-40. Retrieved from Business Source Premier database.

CHAPTER 10

1 Papageorge, A. Creativity quotes: Innovation. Innovation Tools, 2005.
http://www.innovationtools.com/Quotes/QuotesDetail.asp?CatID=4

2 Madslien, J. Airbus to Unveil Giant A380 Plane. BBC News, 2005.
http://www.airbus.com/en/presscentre/pressreleases/pressreleases_
items/10_13_05_a380_world_tour.html

3 Clark, N. Airbus Delays New Jumbo Jet a Second Time. *The New York
Times*, 2006.
http://www.nytimes.com/2006/10/03/business/03cnd-airbus.html?ei=5
088&en=5f71b69d505393d0&ex=1317528000&partner=rssnyt&emc=rs
s&pagewanted=print

4 Clark, N. Airbus Replaces Chief of Jumbo Jet Project. *International Herald
Tribune*, 2006.http://www.iht.com/articles/2006/09/04/business/airbus.php

5 Kundnani, H. What's the Problem with Airbus? *The Guardian*, 2006.
http://www.guardian.co.uk/g2/story/0,,1887733,00.html

6 Robertson, D. Airbus Will Lose 4.8 Billion Euros Because of A380
Delays. *Times Online*, 2006.
http://business.timesonline.co.uk/tol/business/industry_sectors/
engineering/article659591.ece

7 Michaels, P. Timeline: iPodding Through the Years. *Playlist Magazine*,
2006. http://playlistmag.com/features/2006/10/ipodtimeline/index.php

8   Cohen, P. and Snell, J. Apple Event: Live Coverage. Macworld, 2007.
    http://www.macworld.com/news/2007/09/04/livecoverage/index.php

9   Christensen, C. M. *The Innovator's Dilemma: When New Technologies Cause Great Firms to Fail.* Massachusetts: Harvard Business School Press, 1997.

10 Presentation by Professor Christensen, C. M. at Nanyang Technological University, Singapore. 2005.

11 IT Facts staff. PC Market Up 18.8% in 2005, Dell the Leader with 18.1%. IT Facts, 2006. http://www.itfacts.biz/index.php?id=P5601

12 The Coca-Cola Company staff. The Chronicle of Coca-Cola. The Coca-Cola Company, 2007. http://www.thecoca-colacompany.com/heritage/chronicle_birth_refreshing_idea.html

13 Hitt, M. A., Hoskisson, R. E., and Ireland, R.D. Managers and Acquisitions and Managerial Commitment to Innovation in M-Form Firms. *Strategic Management Journal.* 1990. Volume 11. Special Issue: Corporate Entrepreneurship, Pgs 29-47. Retrieved from JSTOR database.

14 Slater, R. *Jack Welch and the G.E. Way.* Ohio: McGraw-Hill, 1998.

15 Interbrand staff. Best Global Brands 2006. Interbrand, 2007. http://www.interbrand.com/best_brands_2006.asp

16 Pendergrast, M. *For God, Country and Coca-Cola.* New York: Basic Books Publishing Company, 2000.

17 Singapore Airlines staff. The SIA Story. Singapore Airlines, 2007. http://www.singaporeair.com/saa/en_UK/content/company_info/siastory/history.jsp

18 Singapore Airlines staff. First Class Seat. Singapore Airlines, 2007. http://www.singaporeair.com/saa/en_UK/content/exp/cabin/firstclass_seat.jsp

19 Singapore Airlines staff. Entertainment Devices. Singapore Airlines, 2007. http://www.singaporeair.com/saa/en_UK/content/exp/entertainment/devices/screens.jsp

20 Skytrax staff. Airline Ranking. Skytrax, 2007. website: http://www.airlinequality.com/StarRanking/5star.htm

21 Bureau of East Asian and Pacific Affairs staff. Background Note: Singapore. U.S. Department of State, 2007. http://www.state.gov/r/pa/ei/bgn/2798.htm

22 Singapore Economic Development Board staff. Singapore Economic Development Board, 2007. \ http://www.edb.gov.sg/edb/sg/en_uk/index/about_us/our_history/the_1970s.html

23 International Monetary Fund staff. World Economic Outlook Database. International Monetary Fund, 2007.
    http://imf.org/external/pubs/ft/weo/2007/01/data/weorept.aspx

24 Skytrax staff. Singapore Changi Airport is Crowned the World's Best Airport as the 2006 Airport Awards are Announced. Skytrax, 2006. http://www.airlinequality.com/news/230506-bestairport.htm

25 Wong, J. Singapore Retains Ranking as Busiest Port in 2006. Channel NewsAsia, 2007. http://www.channelnewsasia.com/stories/singaporebusinessnews/view/251730/1/.html

CHAPTER 11

1 Museum Marketing Tips staff. Motivational Quotes: Marketing and Advertising. Museum Marketing Tips. http://www.museummarketingtips.com/quotes/quotes_ac.html

A

Advertising 7, 18-21, 47, 49, 54, 58, 81-82, 94, 97, 100, 102, 108, 113-124, 126, 129, 130, 143, 145, 148-150, 158, 160, 184, 200, 207, 217
  Importance of advertising 113
  One second advertisements 123

Attractiveness 26, 154

B

Barriers 182, 184, 203
  to Entry 184
  to Wowability 182
Blinks 123, 124
Blogging 54, 119-120
Brainstorming 166-167
  Basic Guidelines 167
  Definition 166
  Misconceptions 168-171
Brand Banking 15-24
  Twelve Principles 16-24
Brand bank account 20-23, 26, 198
  Master brand bank 17, 25
  Premium brand bank 23, 38
  Regular brand bank 23, 26, 198

Brand preference ladder 16, 22-24, 76, 108, 198
Brand Proliferation 133
Branding 15, 24, 94-102
  Brand leaders 98-100
  Brand logo 95
  Brand name 95
  Brand story 96-97

C

Celebrity endorsements 115-117
Communications 20-21, 54, 71, 106, 112, 120, 122, 125, 129, 131, 140-141, 145
  Human touch 97
  Feedback 118, 122, 147
  Promoting Achievements
  Mistakes 77, 160, 173
Communicational contact points 111-126
  Definition 111
  The Internet 117-120
    Blogging 119-120
    Online Reviews 117-119
  Three levels 111
    Affective 111
    Behavioral 111
    Cognitive 111
Comparative advertising 18
Contact points 47-54

Choosing 201
Classification 51-54
Communicational 111-126
Emotional 85-102
Functional 63-75
Varying importance 201
Risks 202
Convenience 70-71
Customer Service 89-90
Pre-purchase service 90
Point-of-Purchase service 90, 91
Post-purchase service 91
Curse of knowledge 112

D
Design 100-102
Delight 5-6, 8, 11, 23, 31, 49, 160, 209-210
Disruptive Wowability 184-187

E
Economics of Wowability 31-41
Emotional contact points 85-102
Barriers 184
Definition 85
Improving 53
Expectations 31
Definition 31
Ever increasing 179-180
Exceeding Expectations 5, 7-8, 31, 37-39, 63-64, 86, 142, 144-145, 186, 197, 205, 209, 210
Managing Expectations 180-182, 202-203
Release dates 180-182
Price 203

F
Familiarity 16, 25, 54, 137, 139, 140-141, 144-146, 153-160
FAR Paradigm 153-161
Familiarity 153-154
Attractiveness 154
Reputation 154-155
Relevance 155-156
FAR Paradigm Familiarity Matrix 157
Tough Square 158
Maybe Square 158
Unclaimed Potential Square 158
High Repeat Purchases Square 159
FAR Paradigm Reputation Matrix 159
Tough Square 159
Problem Square 160
Maybe Repeat Purchases 160
Loyal users 160
Fashion 26, 104-106
bags 20
phones 106
Features 65-67
Functional contact points 36, 52, 55, 63-75, 85, 100, 143, 183-184, 190, 200-201, 209

Barriers 184-185
Definition 183-184

H

Halo effect 17, 25, 42, 73, 78, 198
Hiring 90, 114

L

Laddering 165-166
Leadership 41, 47, 53, 81, 105,
    142, 166, 189, 200, 207
Location 71-75
    Product Location and
    Communications Placement
    71-73
    Country of Origin Effect 73-
    75

M

Managing expectations 180-182
Mediocrity 37-40, 151
Mind Mapping 171-172
    Definition 171
    Rough Guide 171-172

O

Online reviews 117-119

P

Packaging 18, 74, 92, 132, 133,
    134, 148, 149
People 5, 7-8, 10, 19, 21, 57-58,
75, 85-86, 90, 96-99, 102, 107-
109, 113, 116, 118, 121, 124-125,
127, 138-139, 147, 163, 166-
168, 170, 173, 183, 193-194
Personality 94, 98, 99
Preference 5, 8, 16, 22-24, 38-39,
    42, 50, 76-77, 79, 91, 103, 108,
    153, 166, 197-199, 207, 209-
    210
Positioning 49-50
Price 87-89
    Dynamic pricing 88-89
    Indicator of quality 87-88
    Value for money 88, 203
    Reference pricing 88
Product placement in Movies
    122-123

Q

Quality 67-70

R

Release Dates 180-182

Reputation 8, 13, 38, 69, 73, 76,
    98, 153, 154-160, 209

S

Satisfaction 95-96, 126, 129, 131,
    155, 170
Survey 8, 38, 63, 86, 91, 137, 138-
    143, 152, 161, 207-209

T

Technology 10, 36, 39, 52, 61, 64-65, 68-69, 79-81, 93-94, 97, 101, 102, 103, 105, 116-168, 174, 175, 183, 185-190, 200

Tools

  Qualitative tools 165-172

    Brainstorming 166-167

    Laddering 165-166

    Mindmapping 171-172

  Quantitative tools 137-161

    Wow score tool 137

      Familiarity 153

      Importance 148, 149

      Inside-out Approach 146

      Outside-in Approach 146

      The right contact points 139

      The right people 139

      The structure 139-141

      Wow score 142-144

      Wowability Test 147-148

      FAR Paradigm 153-160

U

User experience 92

V

Value 31-38

  Functional Value 32-37

  Emotional Value 37-38

W

Word-of-Mouth 120

  How to make it work 121

Wowability 5-10

  Attitude 40-41

  Barriers to 183-184

  Definition 5-9

  Disruptive 185-187

  Qualitative tools 165-172

  Quantitative tools 137-161

  Principles of 197

  Sustaining 39-40, 179-187

  Economics 31-41

  Wow point 201

  Wow score 138-147

  Wowability Zone 38-40

Wowability Framework 211-218

  Existing contact points Matrix 213

  Existing contact points Product Matrix 216

  Existing contact points Resultant Matrix 215

  Existing contact point Weighted Matrix 214

  New contact points Matrix 217

  New contact points Product Matrix 218

  New contact points Resultant Matrix 218

  New contact point Weighted Matrix 217

Pool of contact points 211
Sources 211
Wowability Test 147-161
  How to make use of results
  152-153
  Test Procedure 147-151

Wow Score Tool 138-147
  Efficacy 138
  Inside-out Approach 146
  Outside-in Approach 146
  Structure 139-141
  Wow score 142-144

Brands Index

3M 173-174
7-Eleven 71-72
Adidas 95, 97, 115-117
Airbus 180-181
Amazon.com 13, 89, 117
Apple 5, 21, 39, 42-43, 47,
  49, 64, 86, 98-99, 119, 140,
  142, 154, 181-182, 186, 201,
  207, 208, 209
AXE 107-108
Ben & Jerry's 39, 63-64, 86,
  93, 97, 132-134
BMW 50, 65, 74, 78, 89, 102,
  204-205
Budweiser 113, 114
Chery 50, 52
Coca-Cola 5, 7, 9, 18-19, 39,
  48, 63-64, 86, 88-89, 96,
  126-132, 155, 187, 189-190,
  209
Creative ZEN 140-142, 207
David Beckham 115
Dell 9, 39, 64, 86, 96, 185, 209
Deuter 69

eBay 131
E.T. 11
General Electric 100, 186-190
Gillette 70, 115
Google 39, 64, 80-82, 86, 209
Haägen-Dazs 74, 93
Harley Davidson 34-35
IBM 75, 167-168, 185-186
iPod 7, 21, 39, 42-43, 49-50,
  64, 85-86, 140-143, 181-182,
  207-209
Johnnie Walker 115
Kentucky Fried Chicken 96-
  97
LG 24
Lenovo 39, 64, 74-75, 86, 116,
  185, 209
Lexus 39, 64, 74-76, 78-79, 86,
  89, 94, 209
Louis Vuitton 20, 49
McDonald's 8, 18-19, 39, 64,
  71, 86, 190, 209
Microsoft 5, 126
Motorola 24, 70, 93, 103,
  175-176

Muji 8

Nokia 5, 7, 18, 24, 37, 39, 64, 66, 86, 93-94, 103-107, 119, 209, 212, 214

Nordstrom 90

Old San Francisco 9-10

Pixar 98

Prius 32, 36-37, 76, 78-79

Ronaldinho 116

Samsung 5, 17, 24, 25-27, 39, 40-41, 64, 75, 86, 93-94, 209

Singapore 50, 193-194, 207

Singapore Airlines 39, 64, 86, 179-181, 187, 191-193, 202, 209

Sony 17, 75, 140, 142, 186, 207, 208

Starbucks 5, 7, 9, 23, 32, 39, 48, 54-59, 64, 71, 83, 85-86, 204, 209

Steve Jobs 5, 20, 47, 97-99

Steven Spielberg 10-11, 98

Toyota 5, 36-37, 39, 50, 64, 74-79, 86-87, 92, 207

Virgin 5, 98, 163

Volkswagen 102

Wal-Mart 49, 72, 90, 105

Wow Stories Index

Steven Spielberg 10-11

Samsung 25-27

Apple 42-43

Starbucks 54-59

Toyota 76-79

Google 80-82

Nokia 103-107

AXE 107-108

Coca-Cola 126-132, 189-190

Ben & Jerry's 132-134

IBM 167-168

3M 173-174

Motorola 175-176

General Electric 187-189

Singapore Airlines 190-192

Singapore 192-194